Judaism

A Beginner's Guide

ONEWORLD BEGINNER'S GUIDES combine an original, inventive, and engaging approach with expert analysis on subjects ranging from art and history to religion and politics, and everything in between. Innovative and affordable, books in the series are perfect for anyone curious about the way the world works and the big ideas of our time.

anarchism	french revolution
aquinas	history of science
artificial intelligence	humanism
the beat generation	islamic philosophy
biodiversity	journalism
bioterror & biowarfare	lacan
the brain	life in the universe
the buddha	literary theory
censorship	machiavelli
christianity	mafia & organized crime
civil liberties	magic
classical music	marx
climate change	medieval philosophy
cloning	middle east
cold war	NATO
conservation	the northern ireland conflict
crimes against humanity	oil
criminal psychology	opera
critical thinking	the palestine–israeli conflict
daoism	philosophy of mind
democracy	philosophy of religion
dyslexia	philosophy of science
energy	postmodernism
engineering	psychology
the enlightenment	quantum physics
evolution	the qur'an
evolutionary psychology	racism
existentialism	renaissance art
fair trade	the small arms trade
feminism	sufism
forensic science	

Judaism

A Beginner's Guide

Lavinia and Dan Cohn-Sherbok

ONEWORLD
OXFORD

A Oneworld Book

First published by Oneworld Publications as
Judaism: A Short Introduction, 1997
First published in the *Beginner's Guide* series 2010

ISBN 978–1–85168–748–0

Typeset by Jayvee, Trivandrum, India
Cover design by vaguelymemorable.com
Printed and bound in Great Britain by CPI Cox & Wyman, Reading

Oneworld Publications
UK: 185 Banbury Road, Oxford OX2 7AR, England
USA: 38 Greene Street, 4th Floor, New York NY 10013, USA
www.oneworld-publications.com

Contents

13 **Death and mourning** 154

Introduction

Recorded Jewish history extends at least from the time of King David three thousand years ago. From then to the present day, Jews have formed a tiny percentage of the world's population, yet their influence has been incalculable. Nearly two thousand years ago, Judaism's great daughter religion, Christianity, began. Later, the Jewish people were to be a significant influence on Muhammad. Meanwhile, the Jews continued to worship God in their own way: they developed their own laws, followed their own liturgy and maintained their own separateness.

Through their scriptures, known to Christians as the Old Testament, Jews gave the world ethical monotheism. The scriptures give a particular vision of history; it starts with creation, incorporates individual and community destiny and will conclude with divine–human reconciliation. This scheme was, for centuries, fundamental to Western thinking. It was the Jews who equated God's will with social justice and who insisted that divine law was the platform on which civilized human society must rest.

Their contribution has not only been religious. Between CE 70 and 1948, the Jews had no country of their own, living among other nations and developing their own patterns of organization and government. All too often they were regarded as a strange, sinister minority by their host nations. Much of Jewish history involves persecution, exile, discrimination and martyrdom. Yet the Jewish community did much for their new countries, particularly in the economic sphere, establishing international trading links and helping organize rudimentary banking systems. In addition they fought in the armies and were known for their skill in medicine and crafts.

Once the many civil disabilities from which they suffered were removed and they were permitted to benefit from mainstream education, many Jewish individuals became detached from their religious roots. A remarkable number of the leading thinkers of the nineteenth and twentieth centuries were of Jewish origin: the economist David Ricardo, the political theorist Karl Marx, the British politician Benjamin Disraeli, the revolutionary Leon Trotsky, the philosopher Ludwig Wittgenstein, the physicist Albert Einstein, the sociologist Émile Durkheim, the psychiatrist Sigmund Freud, the linguist Noam Chomsky, the anthropologist Claude Lévi-Strauss, the literary critic Jacques Derrida and the film-maker Woody Allen, to name but a few. This group has helped to transform the way we look at the world. Not one of them was religious in the traditional sense, but all were deeply influenced by Jewish beliefs and attitudes.

This book is an attempt to explain the Jewish religion as it is practised today. The first six chapters are concerned with theology. They discuss the nature of God, the role of the Jewish people in God's creation, the divisions within Judaism, the place of the land of Israel in God's scheme, the future hope and the relationship between Judaism and the other great religions of the world. The last seven chapters describe Jewish practice. They discuss Jewish worship, the festivals, the fast days, the ceremonies of childhood and youth, the ceremonies of adulthood, the laws of everyday living and the Jewish way of death and mourning.

The work is intended as a companion volume to the authors' *A Short History of Judaism* and *A Short Reader in Judaism*. As in these books, the abbreviations BC and AD have been replaced with the more widely accepted BCE (Before Common Era) and CE (Common Era). Biblical quotations are from the Revised

Standard Version. The book ends with a short list of suggested books on the relevant topics. In addition, the reader is recommended to consult one of the excellent encyclopaedias of Judaism listed below:

Encyclopaedia Judaica, Macmillan Reference USA, 2006.

Louis Jacobs, *The Jewish Religion: A Companion*, Oxford, 1995.

Geoffrey Wigoder, *The New Standard Jewish Encyclopaedia*, rev. edn; Jerusalem, 1992.

The Encyclopaedia of Judaism, Jerusalem, 1989.

1
The nature of God

Unity

The primary belief of Judaism is that God is One. He is a single unity, undivided, indivisible and unique. The first prayer of the Jewish faith is a declaration of this conviction: 'Shema Israel, Adonai Eloheynu, Adonai Ehad!' (Hear O Israel, the Lord our God, the Lord is One!). This is recited several times during the synagogue daily services and traditionally it is said before going to bed at night and on rising in the morning. Every pious Jew hopes to be able to say it on his or her deathbed. It is the supreme truth, the crucial theological insight which the Jews have given to the world.

Many verses in the Hebrew scriptures affirm the oneness of God. Through the prophet Isaiah, God declares, 'I am the Lord and there is no other, besides Me there is no God' (Isaiah 45:5). In the book of Deuteronomy, supposedly given to Moses, God says, 'See now that I, even I am He, and there is no God beside Me' (32:39) and earlier in the same book He remarks, 'To you it was shown that the Lord is God, there is no one other besides Him' (4:35).

In biblical times the battle was against paganism. The surrounding peoples believed in many gods, all of whom had different attributes and different spheres of interest. They were very much like glorified human beings. They desired each other; they gave birth; they feasted together; they quarrelled with each other; they had battles and they made new alliances. The Jewish God is not like that. Such verses as 'Who is like Thee, O Lord, among the Gods? Who is like Thee, majestic in holiness, terrible in glorious deeds' indicate His qualitative difference. Unlike the pagan gods who are merely the heroes of their particular area of competence, the Jewish God is the ultimate subject. He is the cause of everything that is, the source of all existence, the single perfect being.

Today the challenge to the Jewish view of God comes not from paganism, but from atheism. To many people nowadays the heavens seem empty. Science seems to have provided an alternative model of the universe. It is not governed by a supreme being, but by the immutable laws of cause and effect. Apples fall to the ground because of the laws of gravity; human beings catch infectious diseases because they have been exposed to germs; thunderstorms are the result of conflicting pressures in the atmosphere. Like the other great religions of the world in the twentieth century, Judaism is under siege from scientific atheism. But for most of its long history, it flourished in a believing culture and atheism was not a realistic option.

More of a threat came from dualism and trinitarianism. Dualism is the belief that there are not one but two ultimate powers in the universe, light and darkness, good and bad. This was the view of the Zoroastrians (today's Parsees) and it is an attractive creed in that it solves the problem of how a good God tolerates evil in the world He has made. Nonetheless it was unequivocally rejected by the prophets. As Isaiah put it: 'I form light and create darkness. I make weal and create woe. I am the Lord who do all these things' (45:7). The trinitarianism of Christianity was also repudiated. Christians insist that they do believe in one God – He just happens to be manifest in three persons. Jews feel this is an equivocation and that the Christian creed is a rejection of the essential truth of God's oneness.

The belief in God's unity is splendidly expressed in a poem of the eleventh-century philosopher Solomon ben Joseph ibn Gabirol:

> Thou art One, the beginning of all counting, the base of all
>   construction,
> Thou art One, and in the mystery of Thy Oneness, the wise are
>   astonished, for they know not what it is.
> Thou art One, and Thy Oneness neither diminishes nor
>   increases, neither lacks nor exceeds.
> Thou art One, but not as the one that is counted or owned,
>   for number and chance, nor attribute nor form, can reach
>   Thee.[1]

The names of God

The Jewish God is not merely a philosophical concept, a final
cause which explains the existence of the universe. He is a
personal God – the true hero of the biblical stories and the guide
and mentor of His Chosen People. As such He has a proper
name. In the Hebrew scriptures that name is written as יהוה,
since Hebrew script originally contained no vowels. God's name
was almost certainly pronounced in early times, but by the third
century BCE the consonants were regarded as so sacred that they
were never articulated. Instead, the convention was to read the
letters as *Adonai*, which means 'Lord'. Thus in English translations of the Hebrew text, יהוה is never written as a proper
name, but as 'the Lord'.

יהוה is explained in the book of Exodus as 'I AM WHO I
AM' and it is clearly derived from the old Hebrew verb היה
which means 'to be'. The term 'Jehovah' was introduced by
Christian scholars. It is merely יהוה pronounced with the
vowels of *Adonai* – thus making JeHoVaH. It is a hybrid and is
not usually used by Jews. Over the course of time, even the title
Adonai was regarded as too awesome to represent the four letters
of God's name and today most Orthodox Jews use *Ha-Shem*,
which simply means 'the Name'. Terms for God are treated

with the greatest reverence. Among the strictly traditional, even English translations are perceived as too holy to write and today the custom is to inscribe G-d, the L-rd and even the Alm-ghty. This carefulness is explained and justified by the prohibition in the Ten Commandments: 'You shall not take the name of יהוה your God in vain; for יהוה will not hold him guiltless who takes His name in vain' (Exodus 20:7).

In ancient times the term *Adonai* was not just used for God. It was a common mode of address to kings, slave-masters and even by wives to husbands. The 'i' at the end signifies 'my'. And, in fact, *Adona* is a plural form so it literally means 'my lords'. In many verses of scripture and in the liturgy, God is spoken of as יהוה (pronounced *Adonai*) *Eloheynu*, which means 'the Lord our God'.

In the Bible, God has many other names. He is often described as *Elohim*, which simply means God. It is in fact, a plural form and is also, on occasions, used to refer to the pagan gods. When referring to the One Jewish God, the form *Ha-Elohim* (the God) is often employed. Various conjectures have been made as to why a plural noun should be used to designate the unity of the One God. It has been suggested that it is a final remnant of archaic polytheistic beliefs or even that it indicates the importance of the deity – as in the 'royal we'. Most scholars, however, think that it was taken from the Canaanite language. The Canaanites were the indigenous people of the land of Israel and they seem frequently to have addressed their individual gods as 'my gods'.

The Canaanite word for god was *El*. This is not used often in the Bible except when it is coupled with another title. God is sometimes called *El Elyon* – literally God Most High. So the Psalmist declares, 'I will give thanks to the Lord with my whole heart ... I will sing praises to Thy name O Most High' (Psalm 9:1–2) and 'Let them know that Thou alone whose name is יהוה art the Most High over all the world' (Psalm 83:18). Like the term *Elohim*, this title was taken over from the Canaanites who traditionally described *El Elyon* as the lord of all the gods. When the Jews took possession of the Promised Land, it was natural enough for them also to adopt this title for their One God.

Similar borrowings occurred with *El Olam* (the Everlasting God) and *El Shaddai* (the Almighty God). The book of Genesis describes the patriarch Abraham calling God *El Olam* at the shrine of Beersheba: 'Abraham planted a tamarisk tree in Beersheba and called there on the name of יהוה, the Everlasting God' (21:33). Similarly, when Abraham attained the age of ninety-nine, יהוה appeared to him and said, 'I am God Almighty, walk with me and be blameless' (17:1). In both instances there are clear Canaanite connections. Beersheba was almost certainly an old pagan shrine and, when God revealed Himself as *El Shaddai*, He was promising the patriarch that the land of Canaan (the Promised Land) was to be given to his descendants for ever.

It is notable that even today many Hebrew personal names incorporate the names of God. Dani*el*, Micha*el*, *El*isha, Isra*el*, and Ezeki*el* are all built round *El*. *El*ijah uses both El and יהוה while *Adonijah* grows from יהוה and Adonai. The same is true of many modern Israeli surnames, as in that of Prime Minister Binyamin Netan*yah*u, which is clearly derived from the proper name of God.

The attributes of God

God's names reflect His attributes. First of all, He is eternal. Throughout the Hebrew scriptures, He is described as having neither a beginning nor an end. As the Psalmist put it: 'Before the mountains were brought forth, or ever Thou hadst formed the earth and the world, from everlasting to everlasting, Thou art God' (Psalm 90:2). Thus God is fundamentally different and other from His creation. He lies outside it, so to speak. He is the one constant against which the ephemera of the universe passes. Everything in the physical world is subject to the laws of birth and death, renewal and decay. God alone is unchanging.

In later rabbinic interpretations of scripture, this idea is elaborated: 'The power and might of our God fill the world. He was before the world was created and He will be when all the world comes to an end.'[2] In general, however, philosophical speculation was discouraged. According to the Mishnah, the second-century collection of oral law, 'whoever reflects on four things, it were better for him that he had not come into the world: What is above? What is below? What is before? What is after?' Nonetheless, in later centuries, Jewish philosophers did try to come to some sort of understanding of the concept of eternity. In general, the consensus was that God lived in a sphere outside time, in an eternal present. Thus the thirteenth-century theologian Bahya ibn Asher ibn Halawa declared that 'all times past and future are in the present so far as God is concerned, for He was before time and is not encompassed by it'.[3] The eternity of the Almighty is accepted as an article of the Jewish faith. In the liturgy He is described as 'the Lord of the Universe, who reigned before any creature yet was formed and, at the time when all things shall come to an end, He alone will reign'.[4]

Connected with the belief in God's eternity is the conviction that He is omniscient – that He knows everything. As the Psalmist wrote: 'O Lord, Thou hast searched me out and known me. Thou knowest when I sit down and when I rise up; Thou discernest my thoughts from afar. Thou searched out my path and my lying down, and art acquainted with all my ways' (Psalm 139:1–3). This is only to be expected in a God who is outside time. Since the past and the future are in an eternal present to Him, His knowledge is not limited by space or time.

The rabbis were aware that this raises the problem of human freedom. If God knows exactly what you will do tomorrow (since He is experiencing it in His eternal present), it is hard to see how you could do otherwise. Nonetheless the sages insisted that human beings do have real liberty. Rabbi Akiva, the most prominent authority of the late first/early second century, flatly declared: 'All is foreseen, but freedom of choice is given.'[5] Later philosophers were not so sure and offered alternative explanations. In the twelfth century, Maimonides insisted that God's knowledge was different from that of human beings and humans simply cannot understand its nature. Gersonides, in the early fourteenth century, maintained that God only knows things in general and He understands the full range of possibilities facing human beings. However, He does not know which possibility people will in fact adopt. On the other hand, Hasdai Crescas of the late fourteenth century argued that God's knowledge is absolute and human free will is nothing more than an illusion.

Connected with the attribute of omniscience is that of omnipotence. Nothing is said to be impossible with God. As He Himself declared in the book of Jeremiah, 'Behold I am the Lord of all flesh: is anything too hard for me?' (32:27). This also raises philosophical problems. Most Jewish thinkers were convinced that God was not capable of effecting the logically impossible. It was generally accepted that He could not defy the laws of mathematics or change the past. Nonetheless they insisted that this showed no deficiency in God's guidance of the universes and, in all other matters, God could accomplish anything.

In recent times, these attributes of omnipotence and omniscience have raised a seemingly insoluble problem in the light of the Holocaust. If God knows everything, He must have been aware that six million of His Chosen People were being murdered in unspeakable circumstances. If He is all-powerful then He could have prevented the whole ghastly episode. How then can we account for His inactivity? As yet this overwhelming conundrum has not been solved.

God the creator

According to the book of Genesis in the Hebrew scriptures, God is the source of the universe.

> In the beginning, God created the heavens and the earth. The earth was without form and void and darkness was upon the face of the deep: and the Spirit of God was moving over the face of the waters. And God said, 'Let there be light'; and there was light. And God saw that the light was good; and God separated the light from the darkness. God called the light Day and the darkness he called Night. And there was evening and there was morning, one day. (1:1–5)

The narrative continues to explain how God laboured for six days. He made the heavens, the seas and the earth. Then He made the earth bring forth every kind of vegetation for food; He created the sun, the moon and the stars and He brought into being all the sea-creatures, birds, insects and mammals. Finally He declared:

> 'Let us make man in Our image, after Our likeness, and let them have dominion over the fish of the sea and over the birds of the air and over the cattle and over all the earth and over every creeping thing that creeps over the earth.' So God created man in His own image, in the image of God He created him; male and female He created them. (Genesis 1:26–7)

This belief in God the creator has become a central feature of the synagogue liturgical service. The congregation declares, 'I believe with perfect faith that the Creator, blessed be His Name, is the author and guide of everything that has been created, and that He alone has made, does make and will make all things.' So creation is not merely seen as a historical event of the distant past. God is not like some celestial watchmaker who produces a magnificent piece of clockwork, winds it up and then leaves it to run down by itself. Instead, He is intimately involved in the world that He has made – every new leaf, each change in the seasons, every fresh nestling is evidence of the ongoing process of divine creation.

Jews conceive of God as both transcendent and immanent. Scripture repeatedly affirms this. On the one hand, 'My thoughts are not your thoughts, neither are your ways My ways, says the Lord. For as the heavens are higher than the earth, so are My ways higher than your ways and My thoughts higher than your thoughts' (Isaiah 55:8–9). At the same time, He is close to each human being and there is no escape from His reality. As the Psalmist puts it, 'Whither shall I go from Thy Spirit? Or whither shall I flee from Thy presence? If I ascend to Heaven, Thou art there! If I make my bed in Sheol, Thou art there! If I take the wings of the morning and dwell in the utter-most parts of the sea, even then Thy hand shall lead me, and Thy right hand shall hold me' (Psalm 139:7–10). Rabbi Levi Yitzhak of Berditchev, a mystic of the late eighteenth/early nineteenth centuries, made the same point in a poem:

> Where I wander – You! Where I ponder – You!
> Only You, You again, always You! You! You! You!
> When I am gladdened – You! When I am saddened – You!
> Only You, You again, always You! You! You! You![6]

Judaism, then, teaches both that God is beyond and outside the universe and that He is closely involved in every detail of it. Human beings are the crown of His creation. They alone, both men and women, are in the image of God and can share in the creative process through their dominion over the plants and creatures of the earth. With the expansion of modern scientific knowledge, these doctrines have been called into question. Charles Darwin's theory of evolution by natural selection indicates that human beings have, over an immense period of time, evolved from other creatures and that there is no obvious qualitative difference between humanity and the rest of the natural world. Men and women are merely the most intelligent creatures to have so far evolved. It is also quite possible that other forms of intelligent life will be found on other, as yet undiscovered, planets. If this is the case, it is hard to insist on the uniqueness of human beings and on God's close involvement in their affairs.

Nonetheless, these conjectures have not disturbed the faith of the pious. The belief that God is the source of all continues to animate religious sensibility. Without ignoring or putting aside scientific explanations, for many the heavens still declare the glory of God and the firmament shows His handiwork.

God and evil

According to the book of Genesis, when God created the universe, He saw that it was good. It was perceived as a reflection of His nature. The world was good because He is good. In the Psalms particularly, His goodness is frequently glorified: 'Thou art my God, and I will give thanks to Thee: Thou art my God, I will extol Thee. O give thanks to the Lord for He is good; for His steadfast love endures for ever' (Psalm 118:28–9). Similarly, 'The Lord is gracious and merciful, slow to anger and abounding in steadfast love. The Lord is good to all, and His compassion is over all that He has made' (Psalm 145:8–9).

In the rabbinic literature, the same view is upheld. God is described as the supremely benevolent creator. He is the father of all and He guides everything that He has made to its ultimate destiny. He is a God of goodness and loving-kindness, who 'makes Peace in the highest Heavens'.[7] Such an affirmation of faith in His goodness raises the question of the origin of evil in the world. Throughout Jewish history, the sages have engaged in intense speculation about these matters.

As has been pointed out earlier, dualism, the doctrine that there are two ultimate powers in the universe, was rejected. God is One. He is the all-knowing, all-powerful, all-good creator. And yet there is evil in the world. Abraham ibn Daud, a philosopher of the twelfth century, realized that since God does not have a composite nature, it is logically impossible for Him to be the source of both good and evil. He solved the problem by arguing that evil is not a quality. It is merely an absence of good. Just as darkness is an absence of light and poverty an absence of wealth, so evil is the result of the non-presence of good. It was not willed by God. It is simply a gap in the goodness created by God.

During the late Middle Ages, Jewish mystics evolved further complicated explanations for the existence of evil in the universe. They taught that God is absolute perfection in which there is no distinction or plurality. He reveals Himself through a series of emanations through which divine energy flows from the highest to the lowest. According to Isaac Luria, an important mystic of the sixteenth century, creation occurred through the contraction of God into Himself. This left an empty space through which God's emanations could flow. But during the process, disaster occurred when the separate elements of the creative forces refused to co-operate. This splintering of the divine purpose brought into being demonic forces which are sustained by the fragments of divine light which they still contained.

Such difficult, esoteric doctrines never became part of the formal religious system. They were shrouded in secrecy and passed down in whispers from master to disciple. Most people struggled to maintain their belief in God's goodness in the face of all the meaningless evil of the world as a matter of faith. Among the less well educated, there was a strong folk belief in demons; amulets were often worn and were hung in Jewish houses to ward off these evil spirits. This kind of superstition has largely disappeared from mainstream Judaism and it was never perceived as an integral part of the religion.

In recent times, Jewish theologians have been forced to grapple with the question of whether it is still possible to believe in the goodness of God after the horrors of the Holocaust. There have been attempts to understand the deaths of the six million as a form of sacrifice – as an acting out of the Jewish role of the suffering servant of God. According to the prophet Isaiah, God's servant would bring salvation to humanity through his anguish. Others have seen coming out of the death camps a divine command that Jews and Judaism must survive at all costs. For the majority, however, it is an insoluble problem. When Job in the Bible was struck down by a terrible series of disasters, he demanded an explanation of God. God's response was, 'Where were you when I laid the foundations of the earth?' (Job 38:4). God's ways are inscrutable. Humanity cannot hope to understand them, and the problem of evil must remain the ultimate theological mystery.

2

The covenant

The chosen people

The Jews believe that they are the Chosen People of God, and this is an essential element in their faith. According to the book of Deuteronomy, 'You are a people holy to the Lord your God; the Lord your God has chosen you to be a people for His own possession out of all the peoples that are on the face of the earth' (7:6). The text goes on to stress that the Jews were selected not because they were the most numerous group, but because 'the Lord loves you and is keeping His oath which He swore to your father' (Deuteronomy 7:8). This is echoed in the traditional synagogue liturgy: 'Thou hast chosen us from all peoples: Thou hast loved us and found pleasure in us and has exalted us above all tongues.'[1]

However, chosenness is not merely a privilege. It carries immense responsibility. Jews believe that they are in a covenant relationship with God. A covenant is a mutual obligation; it is a bargain freely entered into by both parties. In the case of God's covenantal relationship with Israel, the deal is spelled out in the book of Exodus: 'If you will obey My voice and keep My covenant, you shall be My own possession among all peoples' (19:5). In other words, chosenness carries with it the obligation to keep the law of God.

Although the rabbis strongly maintained the doctrine of the Chosen People, they were not always easy with it. Stories were circulated of how God offered the privilege to other nations first. Each time He stressed that being chosen involved keeping all the provisions of the sacred law. In every case, the nations rejected God because they were wedded to their own particular ways of life. Eventually, according to one source, God was compelled to threaten. He is said to have announced that if they accepted His law, all would go well, but if they rejected it, then they would be destroyed there and then. This negative view of chosenness is reflected in the old Jewish joke, which carries with it the accumulated bitterness of the effects of centuries of anti-Semitism: 'O Lord, Thou hast chosen us from among all the peoples – isn't it time you chose someone else?'

However, the majority of authorities taught that that the Jews, who alone accepted the conditions of the covenant, did so joyfully. According to the book of Exodus, when Moses read the Book of the Covenant, the people said, 'All that the Lord has spoken we will do, and we will be obedient' (24:7). The clear connection between keeping the law and being God's Chosen People, again, is spelled out in the liturgy. In the synagogue, when each individual is called up to read from the holy scroll, he recites, 'Blessed art Thou O Lord our God, King of the Universe, who hast chosen us from all peoples and hast given us Thy Law.'[2]

Thus the selection of the Jews reflects not only God's generous outpouring of love, but also His determination that His law should be observed. This raises the problem of what happens when the Jewish people are unfaithful to the covenant. In the real world, when one party breaks one side of a contract, there are penalty clauses and the contract may become null and void. Could this happen to the Jews? Among all the biblical writers, the prophets of the eighth century BCE were the most exercised by this dilemma. There was no question that the Jewish people had been unfaithful to God. On the one hand, the prophet Hosea wrote, 'The Lord said: Call his name Not-My-People, for you are not my people and I am not your God' (1:9). On the other hand, it was inconceivable that God could give up His Chosen entirely. Drawing on his own experience of an unhappy marriage, Hosea realized that God, like a forbearing husband, would forgive His people again and again: 'How can I give you up O Ephraim; how can I hand you over O Israel! ... My heart recoils within me, My compassion grows warm and tender' (11:12). It does seem that God's love for the Jews ultimately overrides the demand that they keep His law.

This doctrine of chosenness has not made the Jews popular. Almost from its inception, the Christian Church has taught that the Jews have forfeited their special position by their rejection of Jesus as their Messiah. Even today the persistence of the belief that they are the Chosen People is seen as a disguised form of racism. Perhaps the world's ambivalence is best summed up by Hilaire Belloc's cruel little couplet, 'How odd of God, To choose the Jews!' The only response to this can be the well-known, but anonymous, rejoinder, 'It isn't odd, The Jews choose God!'

Revelation

The word for law in Hebrew is *torah*. This term is frequently used for the whole body of revelation which God imparted to His Chosen People. It is an article of the Jewish faith that the Torah came from God. According to the book of Exodus in the Hebrew scriptures, 'The people stood afar off, while Moses drew near to the thick darkness where God was. And the Lord said to Moses, "Thus you shall say to the people of Israel ... Now these are the ordinances which you shall set before them"' (20:21–2; 21:1).

According to the tradition, the biblical figure of Moses, who led the Jews out of slavery in Egypt, is unique in the history of humanity. He is the only person to whom God used to speak 'face to face, as a man speaks to a friend' (Exodus 33:11). The Jews believe that the Torah which Moses handed on to their ancestors in the wilderness was (and is) the authentic word of God. The twelfth-century philosopher Maimonides expressed the matter thus: 'I believe with perfect faith that the prophecy of Moses our teacher ... is true; and that he was the chief of the prophets who preceded him and of all who succeeded him. I believe with perfect faith that the whole and complete Torah as we now have it, is one and the same as that given to Moses ... I believe with perfect faith that the Torah will never be changed, nor that any other law will be given in its place by the creator.'[3]

The rabbis made an important distinction between the revelation of the Pentateuch (the biblical books of Genesis, Exodus, Leviticus, Numbers and Deuteronomy) and that of the rest of the Bible. They explained that the Pentateuch was given immediately by God while the other books were inspired less directly by the Holy Spirit through the prophets. Traditionally the Hebrew scriptures are divided into three sections. The Pentateuch is the Torah; the historical and prophetic books are the Neviim ('Prophets') and the rest are the Ketuvim ('Writings'). Collectively they are commonly known as the Tanakh – an acronym of Torah, Neviim and Ketuvim.

It is therefore the Pentateuch that is held in the most reverence. The central focus of the Sabbath morning service is the taking out of the Torah scroll from the Ark and the ceremonial reading from it. The Ark is the alcove cupboard built in the synagogue wall which is nearest to Jerusalem. It is the focal point of worship and is often richly decorated. The Torah itself is written by hand on lengths of vellum or parchment. These are sewn together to form a long roll. Each end is attached to a wooden stave and, when not in use, it is kept rolled up in an elaborately ornamented cover. Over this is often placed a silver crown to indicate the role of the Torah in the life of the Jewish community. The entire text is divided into fifty-four portions, one of which is read out to the listening congregation every week. The scroll itself is treated with the greatest respect;

the congregation stands when it is taken out of the Ark and
the people bow when it is carried round the synagogue in
procession.

The liturgy itself reflects the importance of the revelation to
Moses:

> Blessed be He who gave the Torah to His people Israel in His
> Holiness. The Torah of the Lord is perfect, refreshing the soul;
> the testimony of the Lord is lasting, making the simple wise; the
> rules of the Lord are just, rejoicing the heart; the command-
> ments of the Lord are clear, enlightening the eyes ... And this is
> the Torah which Moses put before the Children of Israel, as
> commanded by the Lord, through the hand of Moses; it is the
> tree of life to those who grasp it and those who hold it are truly
> happy. Its ways are ways of pleasantness and all its paths are
> peace.[4]

Today many Jews find it difficult to believe that the Torah was
dictated word for word by God to Moses. The findings of
modern biblical scholarship indicate that the Pentateuch was a
composite document, derived from several sources and the
subject of many revisions. Nonetheless the Torah remains the
great treasure. At the very least it represents a way of life which
has sustained the Jewish people for hundreds of years. In a very
real sense the Jews remain a People of the Book.

Written and oral law

Altogether there are 613 commandments in the Pentateuch.
Since Orthodox Jews believe that the Pentateuch was given
directly by God to Moses on Mount Sinai, this means that the
613 commandments were literally dictated by God. They must
be observed in order to keep the covenant. Of the 613, 248 are
positive instructions (for example, 'Be fruitful and multiply') and

365 are prohibitions ('You shall not seethe the kid in its mother's milk'). They cover every aspect of day-to-day life and include the ritual obligations that human beings owe to God.

Best known are the Ten Commandments. These include four ritual laws ('You shall have no other gods before me'; 'You shall not make for yourself a graven image'; 'You shall not take the name of the Lord your God in vain'; and 'Remember the Sabbath day, to keep it holy') and six ethical commands ('Honour your father and your mother'; 'You shall not murder'; 'You shall not commit adultery'; 'You shall not steal'; 'You shall not bear false witness'; and 'You shall not covet'). Taken all in all, these cover the broad sweep of human conduct.

At the same time, much of the Written Law is highly detailed. It is also remarkably humane. To take a random sample from one chapter of the book of Leviticus: 'When you reap the harvest of your land, you shall not reap your field to its very corner ... and you shall not strip your vineyard bare, neither shall you gather the fallen grapes of your vineyard; you shall leave them for the poor' (19:9–10); 'You shall not oppress your neighbour or rob him. The wages of a hired servant shall not remain with you all night until the morning' (19:13); 'You shall not curse the deaf or put a stumbling block before the blind' (19:14); 'The stranger who sojourns with you shall be to you as the native among you and you shall love him as yourself; for you were strangers in the Land of Egypt' (19:34).

There are also many laws concerned with the construction of the tabernacle (the original portable shrine), the conduct of the sacrifices, the organization of the priesthood and the whole pattern of ritual worship. Much of it is no longer relevant today since the Jews are no longer a nomadic people struggling through the wilderness. Their priests largely disappeared with the destruction of the Temple in Jerusalem in CE 70 and sacrifice is specifically forbidden outside the central shrine. Nonetheless the laws are still read Sabbath by Sabbath, year by

year in the synagogue. It was spoken by God and so, in some
sense, it endures forever.

Besides the Written Law, traditional Jews also believe there
is a God-given Oral Law. The term *torah* also includes the laws
that were not written down, but were said to have been passed
down through Moses to the elders, from the elders to the
prophets and from the prophets to the 'Men of the Great
Assembly'. The last of these was Simon the Just. He handed it
down the generations of rabbis until it was finally written down
in the second century CE. The Mishnah, as this great anthology
is called, is a description of rabbinical discussions and a record of
the ritual and ethical decisions reached. Since the law is given by
God, there can be no mistakes. Its precise meaning needs careful
interpretation and it is only through study and debate that the
will of God can be fully discerned.

In later centuries, the sages continued to ponder the implications of the Torah. Their deliberations were recorded in
Palestine in the fourth century CE and in Babylon in the sixth
century. Known as the Talmuds, they describe the discussions of
the authorities on the provisions of the Mishnah. They are huge
compendia of theology, ethics, magic, legend, anecdote and
etiquette as well as law. The study of the Talmud remains the
main focus of traditional Jewish education and it is all-absorbing.

Because of the immensity of the Oral Law, with its majority and
minority opinions and its copious interpretations, later codes were
compiled to summarize the provisions of the law. The best known
of these are the *Mishneh Torah* ('Second Law') of the twelfth-
century philosopher Moses Maimonides and the *Shulhan Arukh*
('Laid Table') written in the sixteenth century by the lega-list Joseph
Caro with a supplement by Moses Isserles (16th century). These
have become the guidebooks to the Orthodox way of life. They
have gone through innumerable editions and have inspired numerous important commentaries. For generations they have been the
cohesive force which has bound the community together.

Belief and practice

The covenant was made with the Jewish people, that is, with the descendants of the Patriarch Abraham. The Jews therefore understand themselves primarily as a nation. Unlike Christianity and Islam, the other great monotheistic religions, adherents do not just see themselves as a faith community. The vast majority of Jews are born as Jews. They are not Jews because they have come to believe in Judaism, but because they happen to share a particular ethnic heritage.

This may explain why, compared with Christianity and Islam, Judaism is far more tolerant of theological diversity. The Talmud itself is a record of debate. There are well-known jokes that where there are four Jews, there are six opinions and that every Jew likes to feel that there is a synagogue which he does go to and another that he would not attend at any price! The sacred texts are traditionally studied by two scholars together so that they can argue out its meaning; it is from a variety of opinion that the truth can be discerned. In any event, the Talmud is primarily about conduct, about how a good Jew should behave in particular circumstances. The codes of Jewish law define the faithful Jew as the one who keeps the commandments. The emphasis is always on correct practice rather than correct belief.

Some authorities have gone so far as to say that the whole idea of Jewish theology is a contradiction in terms because Judaism is intent on performing the will of God, not in defining it. On one level, this contention is absurd. There have been many significant Jewish theologians who have tried to interpret the Jewish religion in the light of the philosophical thinking of their day. At the very least, a basic list would include Philo of Alexandria (c.25 BCE–CE 40), Saadiah Gaon (882–942), Judah Halevi (1074–1144), Maimonides (1135–1204), Gersonides (1288–1344), Hasdai Crescas (c.1340–c.1412), Joseph Albo

(1380–1445), Moses Mendelssohn (1729–86), Franz Rosenzweig (1886–1929) and Leo Baeck (1873–1956).

In addition, there have been attempts to define the essential beliefs of Judaism. The most famous of these is that of Moses Maimonides. His Thirteen Principles of the Jewish Faith have been turned into a hymn and this is frequently sung during the liturgical services. Philo spoke of eight essential principles while Joseph Albo reduced them to three (the existence of God, the divine origin of the Torah and ultimate reward and punishment for the righteous and wicked). At the very minimum, the Jew must surely accept the belief expressed in the oft-repeated declaration, 'Hear O Israel, the Lord our God, the Lord is One.'

Nonetheless, every Jew is part of the covenant independent of his or her attachment to dogma. Jewish belief is decidedly fluid. Christian doctrines were carefully determined at a series of ecclesiastical councils. There has never been a parallel authoritative gathering of rabbis who attempted to summarize the faith. It is notable that Maimonides himself, despite his compilation of the Thirteen Principles, was accused of heresy. All that can be said is that over the centuries a consensus has emerged that there are limits beyond which the explorer has stepped beyond Judaism. Today these limits are very broad. Perhaps only deliberate conversion to another religion places the Jew beyond the covenant – and even then the way is always left open for the wanderer to return to the fold.

There is a famous rabbinical comment on the verse in the book of Jeremiah, 'They have forsaken Me and have not kept My Law' (16:11). The rabbis understood this to mean that God would have preferred His people to have forsaken Him, if only they had kept His commandments. In other words, God is interested in obedience; He is not enthusiastic about theological speculation. The same point is made movingly in a well-known Holocaust story. One evening, amid all the squalor and horror of the concentration camps, a group of pious Jews gathered together. They were going to put God on trial. How could an all-good, all-powerful and all-knowing God tolerate what was happening to His Chosen People? All night the debate raged back and forth. In the end there could be only one possible conclusion. There is no God. The Heavens are empty. The evil of the concentration camps could exist because there was no one to stop it. The Jewish religion was based on a fallacy. When the discussion was finished the dawn was breaking. Another day of brutal, back-breaking work lay ahead. All the participants stood up and they all prayed the traditional morning service together.

The Jewish mission

When Moses was given the Torah, God promised that His Chosen People would have a particular role in His plan for the world: 'Now therefore, if ye will obey My voice indeed and keep My covenant, then ye shall be a particular treasure unto Me above all people: for all the earth is Mine. And ye shall be unto Me a kingdom of priests, and an holy nation' (Exodus 19:5–6). Through the keeping of the Torah, the Jewish people would somehow bring the knowledge of God to humanity.

This does not mean that the Jews had a mission to spread the Torah in its full glory and complexity to the other nations. The rabbis consistently taught that, although non-Jews were not expected to keep all the provisions of the law, there was still a place for the righteous gentile in the world to come. For a Jew to be pleasing to God, he or she must walk in the ways of Torah. For the rest of the world, it has always been enough to keep a few basic moral laws, such as avoiding murder, incest, adultery and idolatry. These laws could be found by the unaided use of human reason.

So although the Torah is God's special gift, keeping its every provision is not necessary for the vast majority of the world's population. Nonetheless, the Torah has cosmic significance. From ancient times the rabbis taught that it was created and dwelt in Heaven with God long before the foundation of the earth. For example, it was said that for nearly a thousand years before the universe was formed, the Torah lay in God's bosom and sang His praises with the angels. It was believed that God consulted the Torah before He embarked on the work of creation and Rabbi Akiva, the most famous authority of the early second century CE, used to describe the Torah as 'the precious instrument by which the world was made'.

The Torah must be seen almost as the blueprint for everything that is. Many of the rabbis identified it with Divine Wisdom whose role in the creation is explained in the book of Proverbs: 'When He appointed the foundations of the earth; then I was by Him, as one brought up with Him and I was daily His delight, rejoicing always before Him ... Now therefore hearken unto me, O ye children; for blest are they that keep my ways' (8:29–30, 32). In the light of this vision, 'law' is far too narrow a translation for the word *torah*. Rather, it means 'teaching' or 'instruction' or even 'pattern'. Through the Torah, the Jews have the inestimable privilege of living in harmony with God's creative and sustaining purposes.

The rabbis expressed this view on many occasions. Taking a selection from the 'Ethics of the Fathers', the best-known portion of the Mishnah: 'Upon three things the world is based, upon the Torah, upon the Temple service and upon the practice of charity'; 'The more Torah, the more life'; 'He who has acquired for himself words of Torah, has acquired for himself life in the World-to-Come'; 'If two sit together and interchange words of Torah, the Divine Presence abides between them'; 'Turn the Torah and turn it over again, for everything is in it.'[5]

Through the gift of the Torah, the Jewish people have a

particular mission. They are God's witnesses. The Jews testify to the reality of the One True God and ultimately they believe that it is through their testimony that the world will be transformed. In the book of Isaiah, the final enlightenment of the gentiles is described:

> And it shall come to pass in the last days that the mountain of the Lord's house shall be established at the top of the mountains, and shall be exalted above the hills; and all nations shall flow into it. And many people shall go and say, Come ye, and let us go up to the mountain of the Lord, to the house of the God of Jacob; and He will teach us of His ways, and we will walk in His paths; for out of Zion shall go forth the law, and the Word of the Lord from Jerusalem. (2:2–3)

Every day in the synagogue, pious Jews wait and pray for this final consummation: 'And it is said, And the Lord shall be King over all the earth; in that day shall the Lord be One and His name One.'[6]

3
Divisions within Judaism

Non-religious Jews

When the prophet Jonah was on board ship, sailing for Tarshish, a terrible storm blew up. The sailors were convinced that someone on board was responsible. They drew lots to find the culprit and the lot fell upon Jonah. They questioned him. They said, '"Tell us on whose account this evil has come upon us. What is your occupation? And whence do you come? What is your country? And of what people are you?' And he said to them: 'I am a Hebrew and I fear the Lord, the God of Heaven who made the sea and the dry land"' (Jonah 1:8–9).

In the case of Jonah in the Bible, national identity and religious belief went together and defined each other. But the two do not necessarily coexist. According to Jewish law, an individual is counted among the Jewish people either if she or he has converted to the Jewish religion or if (as in the vast majority of cases) his or her mother is a Jew. This definition goes back early, at least to rabbinic times. In the Mishnah, it is written that 'the son of an Israelite woman is called thy son, but the son by a heathen woman is not called thy son'.[1] Even though individual Jews are described as sons or daughters of their father, as in Isaac son of Abraham, Dinah daughter of Jacob (not son of Sarah or daughter of Leah), the identity of the mother is all-important for Jewish status.

There are sound practical reasons for this. Births in human society are almost invariably witnessed and there is no doubt about who is actually going through labour. Conception is altogether a more mysterious business and, as the old English folk proverb has it, 'It is a wise man who knows his own father.' In addition, among the Jews who were constantly threatened by hostile neighbours, it did mean that a child conceived by a Jewish woman as a result of rape was automatically counted into the fold.

In the past, when Jews lived in their own separate areas and villages and had as little as possible to do with their gentile neighbours, they could preserve both their ethnic identity and their religion. The boys were taught in schools where the curriculum centred round the Bible and the Talmud. The girls could be instructed solely in the arts of kosher home-making and motherhood. There were few outside influences. It was unthinkable to marry outside the faith. Everyone knew everyone else and strict community control could be exercised. Apostasy, rejecting the Jewish religion and converting to another, was rare and shocking. The Jewish religion was an essential part of Jewish identity.

With the advent of the Enlightenment in the late eighteenth/early nineteenth century, this pattern of living was transformed. Once Jews had been granted full civil rights by their host nations they could, in effect, disappear into a larger society. Religious studies no longer dominated education. Children were no longer necessarily sent to Jewish schools. Young people socialized with their non-Jewish school and university friends. Business contacts could be made with gentile counterparts. Intermarriage with non-Jews became an ever-present threat. Today the biggest Jewish communities in the world are found in Israel and North America. World Jewry is thought to approximate fourteen or fifteen million people. Of these, approximately six million live in Israel, and about the same number live in the United States. Despite the traditional abhorrence of intermarriage, more than 50 per cent of young

American Jews who do marry choose to 'marry out'. This is universally regarded as the greatest problem facing the community today, and the religious authorities seem powerless in their attempts to prevent it.

Even among those who have not intermarried, there is widespread disassociation from religious belief. Many individuals who strongly identify with the Jewish people have no connections with the Jewish religion. They do not belong to a synagogue, they do not celebrate Jewish holidays and they make little attempt to educate their children as Jews. Even in the state of Israel, many citizens are determinedly non-religious. They see themselves as Israelis; they are members of the Jewish state; they fight in its army and they defend its borders, sometimes with their lives. But they prefer to spend the Sabbath on the beach rather than in the synagogue and many positively dislike the Orthodox establishment.

Thus in the modern era, Jewish belief and practice are no longer a necessary part of Jewish identity. Even though it is not possible for a non-Jew to become a Jew without religious conversion, the majority of Jews are Jews by birth – and by no means all of them follow the religion of their ancestors.

The Orthodox

Traditionally Jewish life centred around the observance of the law. As we have seen, it was an article of faith that the Torah was given to Moses in its entirety by God. Therefore it must be true in every particular. In handing down the Torah, Moses acted like a scribe, writing from dictation, and thus the whole Pentateuch is literally the word of God. This conviction sustained the Jewish community through many disasters, from the loss of the Temple in CE 70, through the experience of exile and during periods of persecution and massacre. Together with the oneness of God, it was an essential element of the Jewish creed. Today, the findings of biblical criticism and the general scepticism of the times have undermined this view of the Torah. Nonetheless, some remain faithful. Strictly observant Orthodox Jews (known as Heradim) define themselves as those who remain true to the doctrine that the Torah is from Heaven. This has enormous practical consequence on their day-to-day way of life since they follow not only the provision of the Pentateuch, but also all the manifold details of the Oral Law. It means that they must live near one another because mechanical transport is forbidden on the Sabbath and they must walk to synagogue. Many of the men attend synagogue daily and, within the synagogue building, the women sit separately – often in the balcony behind a thick screen.

A large family is regarded as a blessing. Men and women have clearly demarcated roles. A woman must keep a kosher home, following all the complicated food laws. She must look after and sustain her family and dedicate herself to their needs. She is excused from the positive time-bound commandments (such as saying prayers three times a day) to enable her to run her household smoothly. Totally faithful to her husband, she must dress modestly and ensure her daughters do the same. The children attend Jewish schools where boys and girls are taught separately and follow different curricula. First and foremost, the boys must be learned in the law and, after they leave school, they normally attend a yeshiva, a talmudic academy, for several years before embarking on the task of earning a living. Young people marry in their early twenties and the matches are supervised by their elders. It is common for parents to support the newly weds while the young husband finishes his education. Only when life-long habits are established will the new family achieve economic independence.

In fact, even within the Orthodox community, there are varieties of approaches. The Strictly Orthodox (Haredim), as they call themselves, are mainly Jews of Eastern European origin who are trying to reproduce the life their ancestors lived in Russia, Poland or Lithuania. Large numbers have settled in Israel where they exert considerable influence through their own political parties, but there are also groups in most large European and American cities. This group also includes Oriental Jews who trace their origins back to the ancient communities of the East. They have their own synagogues and their own liturgy. They certainly insist that the Torah came directly from God, but they also try to maintain their own particular traditions.

An important new Orthodox group emerged in the nineteenth century under the leadership of Samson Raphael Hirsch (1808–88). He taught that it was possible to remain an Orthodox Jew while being fully conversant with modern culture. His position came to be known as neo-Orthodoxy (or modern orthodoxy). While strictly observant and accepting the doctrine of the divine origin of the Torah, adherents have no hesitation in dressing in current Western fashion and in attending secular universities. The majority of Orthodox synagogues in Great Britain and the United States are of this type and, in some, men and women even sit together. Although the neo-Orthodox often send their children to Jewish schools, girls and boys are educated in the same classroom and follow the same curriculum. Most neo-Orthodox girls would expect to have their own professional careers and it is likely that the number of children in the family is planned.

The Orthodox cannot be regarded as an organized movement and there is a certain amount of quarrelling among the various groups. Nonetheless, they are united both in the conviction that the Torah was given directly by God to Moses and in their unwavering disapproval of more liberal interpretations of Judaism. They have influence far beyond their numerical strength, partly because they are regarded with awe by their more secular co-religionists and partly because they have control of the religious establishment in the State of Israel. Their views are uncompromising. As one Strictly Orthodox rabbi expressed it in conversation to the authors: 'Our opinion is that there are those who are religious and those who are not yet as religious as we would like them to be.'

The Hasidim

The most conspicuous group among the Orthodox are the Hasidim. The word *hasidim* means 'the Pious' and the Hasidim are known for their spiritual devotion. They are immediately recognizable. The men are bearded and wear side-curls which are twisted and tucked behind their ears. They are invariably dressed in black – large black hat worn over small black skull-cap, black jacket, plain black trousers and black shoes and socks. Their shirts are white, buttoned up to the neck and worn without a tie. Issuing forth from the waistband of their trousers are the ritual fringes (tallit katan) which are worn under a shirt. These are generally discreetly tucked into trouser pockets. On the Sabbath, they are even more resplendent. The weekday jacket is exchanged for a long black silk coat, and instead of the everyday trilby a magnificent fur hat may be worn.

Female dress is perhaps less distinctive. In common with all the Orthodox, the women follow the rules of modesty. Their skirts cover their knees; their sleeves extend over their elbows and their necklines are cut high. The married women wear wigs. This is because, according to the law, once a woman is married, she must conceal her hair so she is no longer a temptation to other men. It has become the tradition for a woman to cut off her hair just before her wedding and to cover her head with a wig. This, of course, also makes the monthly visit to the ritual bath easier to manage. Hasidic families tend to be large. Five or six children are not at all unusual.

Hasidism arose in the early eighteenth century in Eastern Europe. Its founder, Israel ben Eliezer (1700–60), who was known as the Baal Shem Tov (the Master of the Good Name), stressed personal piety and mystical worship. In Europe it centred around the courts of the various spiritual leaders, the tsaddikim, who were believed to have extraordinary powers. When a tsaddik died, he was succeeded in the early days by his most prominent disciple. Subsequently, however, it became a hereditary position and was passed down to son, son-in-law or grandson. This did not prevent rivalry. When Tsaddik Mordecai of Chernobil died in 1837, all eight of his sons set themselves up as tsaddikim. The tsaddik is believed to have a special relation-ship with God. His prayers protect his followers, miracles are not unknown and stories of his saintliness are circulated. He is the spiritual leader of his community and the greatest honour for his disciples is to sit at his Sabbath meal and to share in his leftovers. Hasidic worship is characterized by intense joy. The Psalmist's injunction to 'serve the Lord with gladness' is taken literally and on festivals there is dancing and singing which can spill out from the synagogue onto the street.

The European Hasidic dynasties were decimated by the Nazi Holocaust. Nonetheless Hasidism has survived, particularly in the United States and Israel. Today the most prominent groups are the Belz, the Ger, the Satmar and the Lubavitcher Hasidim. The last named is perhaps the best known in that they regard it as their mission to bring their more secular co-religionists back to Torah obedience. Their last tsaddik, Menahem Mendel Schneersohn, was a remarkable person who was believed by many of his followers to be the long-awaited Messiah. When he eventually died in 1994, at a very great age, the movement was in some disarray since he left no son to succeed him.

In the early days, the Hasidim and the more traditional Orthodox strongly disapproved of each other. The traditionalists believed that the new movement was excessive in its enthusiasms. It ignored the traditional hierarchy of the pious and learned; the veneration of the tsaddik was perceived almost as idolatry and the emphasis on mystical joy rather than the diligent study of the Talmud was thought nothing short of heretical. Bills of excommunication were exchanged between the various groups. Children who joined the Hasidim were disowned, communities were split and families divided.

In recent times, however, the traditionalists have made common cause with the Hasidim. Although they follow different liturgies and support their separate institutions, they are united in their abhorrence of the more liberal interpretations of Judaism. Today the Hasidim are equally diligent students of the law. They remain determined proponents of the doctrine of the divine origin of the Torah and are Orthodox in every sense of the word. They are regarded with respect as well as with curiosity. Jonathan Sacks, the Chief Rabbi of the United Hebrew congregations of the Commonwealth, for example, openly acknowledges his spiritual debt to the Lubavitcher Hasidim and sees them as an important and distinctive segment of the Jewish community.

The conservatives and the reconstructionists

Among religious Jews, the great theological divide is between the Orthodox and the non-Orthodox. Non-Orthodox Judaism arose in response to Jewish participation in mainstream, secular civilization. Increasingly, Western European Jews were uncomfortable with the traditional services; many could no longer read Hebrew and some of the ancient doctrines and practices were felt to have no relevance to modern life. Initially liturgical changes were made. Hymns and prayers were offered in German; choral singing was introduced and the services were conducted with less enthusiasm and more decorum. Later, in the mid-nineteenth century, an attempt was made to study the tradition with no religious presuppositions. Taking note of advances in biblical scholarship, many Jews found they could no longer believe that the entire Written and Oral Torah was handed down complete and perfect by God to Moses on Mount Sinai.

Conservative Judaism is essentially an American phenomenon. It arose in reaction to what were perceived as the radical excesses of the Reform movement (see next section). It stands midway between the certainties of Orthodoxy and the liberties of Reform. Less than half of all American Jews affiliate with a synagogue. Of those who do, the largest number belong to the Orthodox, Conservative, and Reform movements. Since the United States has one of the largest Jewish community in the world, the Conservative movement influences a large number of people – possibly as many as a million and a half.

The two founders of Conservative Judaism were Zechariah Frankel (1801–73) and Solomon Schechter (1847–1915). Both understood the Jewish tradition in dynamic terms. They recognized that Judaism had changed through the centuries and that the ultimate source of authority must be the Jewish people themselves. In the light of history, they maintained that some aspects of the tradition are permanent and stand for all time, while others are only meaningful at certain periods. In fact, they never defined precisely which elements fell within which category, but both were committed to unbiased historical research.

Today Conservative Judaism covers a wide variety of beliefs and considerable tensions exist between members of the Rabbinical Assembly, the official association for Conservative rabbis. Nonetheless, in a recent statement, a measure of agreement was reached: 'We all accept the results of modern scholarship. We agreed that historical development of the tradition had taken place, and that the tradition continues to develop. We all agreed on the indispensability of the Halakhah [Jewish law] for Conservative Jews, but a Halakhah which responds to changing times and changing needs' (statement by Rabbi Kassel Abelson, 1985).

Perhaps a concrete example will give a flavour of Conservative thinking. According to traditional law, if a couple are unhappily married, even if they have been divorced by the secular courts, if the husband refuses to give the wife a religious divorce, she is in effect tied. She cannot remarry and all too often this fact has been used by unscrupulous men to blackmail their wives into accepting disadvantageous divorce settlements. Worse still, the wife can be left dangling in an impossible position, neither married nor unmarried. The Orthodox recognize the unfairness of this but, with their attitude to Jewish law, find it difficult to do anything about it. The Reform movement simply declares the law to be outmoded and unfair to women. It allows the woman to remarry with no further ado. The Conservatives, after looking at all the ancient authorities, have recognized that the rabbis of the talmudic period occasionally annulled marriages for social reasons. They have seized upon this precedent and now write into their marriage contracts that if the husband unreasonably refuses to give a religious divorce to his wife, then the marriage will be declared null and void.

In recent years the Conservative movement has spread beyond the United States. In Israel and Great Britain there are now small Conservative organizations known as the Masorti (meaning 'traditional'). Reconstructionism is a new movement which grew out of Conservative Judaism. It was founded by Mordecai Kaplan (1881–1983) who for many years taught at the Conservative Jewish Theological Seminary. He believed that Judaism is a religious civilization not a divinely revealed religion. He defined God not as a supernatural being, but as 'the sum of all the animating, organizing forces and relationships which are forever making a cosmos out of chaos'. Thus Reconstructionism, like Conservative Judaism, retains many traditional Jewish practices, but differs from its parent movement in explaining its theological beliefs in this-worldly terms. Today the movement supports its own rabbinical training college and has established a small network of synagogues. As yet it has scarcely spread beyond North America.

5. Reform and humanistic Jews

Perhaps a further illustration will best clarify the difference between Orthodox, Conservative and Reform Jews. One of the Ten Commandments declares: 'Six days you shall labour and do all your work; but the seventh day is a Sabbath to the Lord your God; in it you shall not do any work' (Exodus 20:9–10). The rabbis of the Mishnah defined the thirty-nine types of work which were forbidden on the Sabbath, and these included lighting a fire. The Orthodox insist that pushing the starter button on a motor car involves igniting a spark and consequently driving or riding in a motorized vehicle is forbidden. On the Sabbath, therefore, they walk to synagogue. Out of respect for Jewish law, the Conservatives also feel that they should walk. On the other hand, perhaps they live far away and it is more important to attend synagogue regularly than to keep every last detail of Sabbath law. So maybe they drive to synagogue, but they leave the car around the corner so it is not obvious to all what they are doing. Reform Jews have no such scruple. The law was made at a time when lighting a fire was a big effort. The whole point of Sabbath law is to have a day of rest. It is far more restful to ride in a car than to trudge round to the synagogue. So they all come in their motor cars and, in a successful synagogue, the car park is full every Sabbath.

The Reform movement arose in early nineteenth-century Germany. Having had the benefit of a Western secular education and mixing freely with gentiles, these German Jews were embarrassed by the traditional worship services. They created a liturgy which was more dignified and more in keeping with Western ideas. They called their houses of worship temples rather than synagogues; they preferred to pray in German rather than Hebrew and they emphasized the ethical and universal ideals of Judaism. They no longer yearned for the restoration of sacrifice in the Jerusalem Temple and they were not comfortable with many of the traditional laws concerning food, clothing and day-to-day living.

As in Conservative Judaism, there are many shades of opinion to be found among Reform Jews. In 1885 a group of American rabbis produced what was called the Pittsburgh Platform in which they declared, 'We accept as binding only [Judaism's] moral laws and such ceremonies as elevate and sanctify our lives and reject all such as are not adapted to the views and habits of modern civilization.' These early Reform leaders saw themselves as the spiritual descendants of the biblical prophets, calling the people back to a more ethical way of life and dispensing with all the old rituals and ceremonies which obstructed rather than contributed to holiness.

In recent years the Reform movement has become more traditional. In Western society generally, there is a greater interest in ethnic roots, and Reform Jews have not been immune to this. Hebrew has been reintroduced into the services; there is passionate interest in the State of Israel and such rituals as bar mitzvahs have been reinstated. Nonetheless Reform Jews remain committed to such principles as the absolute equality of men and women (they even have female rabbis) and they continue to emphasize the moral over the ceremonial aspects of the faith. In many ways modern Reform Jews live lives that are almost identical to those of their gentile neighbours. Apart from celebrating Passover and Hanukkah rather than Easter and Christmas and circumcising rather than christening their sons, the unbiased observer would notice more similarities than differences. They eat the same food; they wear the same clothes; they share the same worldly aspirations and they enjoy the same amusements. Their lives are very different from those of their ancestors in the Jewish villages of Europe.

Humanistic Judaism is a recent offshoot of the Reform movement. It was founded by Rabbi Sherwin Wine (1928–2007) and it extols the humanistic aspects of Judaism. Like the Reconstructionists, Humanistic Jews have abandoned belief in a supernatural deity and, in its manifesto, the Humanistic Federation declares: 'The natural universe stands on its own, requiring no supernatural intervention ... Judaism, as the civilization of the Jews, is a human creation.'[2] Today there are approximately forty thousand Humanistic Jews and the movement is spreading abroad.

4

The State of Israel

The promised land

Since the Jews perceive themselves as a national as well as a religious group, their sense of identity is strongly tied in with their feelings for the land of Israel. From early times, the connection between the Jews and the Promised Land was enshrined in the liturgy. According to the book of Deuteronomy, every Jew must present the first fruits of his produce to God and, as he does so, he must recite the following formula:

> A wandering Aramaean was my father and he went down into Egypt and sojourned there, few in number; and there he became a nation, great, mighty and populous. And the Egyptians treated us harshly and afflicted us and laid upon us hard bondage. Then we cried to the Lord, the God of our fathers, and the Lord brought us out of Egypt with a mighty hand and an outstretched arm, with great terror, with signs and wonders; and he brought us into this place and gave us this land, a land flowing with milk and honey. (26:5–9)

According to the early legends of the Jews, the land was promised to the Jewish people from earliest times. The father of the Jewish people was Abraham. In the book of Genesis it is described how, in obedience to the word of God, he left the prosperous city of Ur to become a nomadic wanderer. In recognition of his faithfulness, God made His first covenant with the

Jewish people. The sign of the covenant was to be circumcision ('Every male among you shall be circumcised' (17:10)), and God promised, 'I will establish My covenant between Me and you and your descendants after you throughout their generations, for an everlasting covenant, to be God to you and to your descendants after you. And I will give to you, and to your descendants after you, the land of your sojournings, all the land of Canaan, for an everlasting possession' (17:7–8).

The narrative sections of the Pentateuch are primarily concerned with the promise and, finally, the journey to the land of Canaan. The pledge to Abraham was passed on to his son Isaac and then to his grandson Jacob. When Isaac blessed his son and sent him away to find a wife among the family of his kinsfolk, he said, 'May He give the blessing of Abraham to you and to your descendants with you, that you may take possession of the land of your sojournings which God gave to Abraham' (Genesis 28:4). In turn, it was passed down to Jacob's twelve sons, the ancestors of the twelve tribes. The Pentateuch describes how Jacob and his twelve sons settled in the land of Egypt, how their descendants were enslaved there and how Moses led them through the wilderness back towards Canaan. During the course of the journey, God gave Moses the Torah, when he was on Mount Sinai. According to the book of Deuteronomy, Moses declared: 'The Lord commanded me at that time to teach you statutes and ordinances, that you might do them in the land which you are going over to possess' (4:14).

In the years that followed, the Jews did establish themselves in the land, but it was not a permanent possession. In the eighth century BCE, the ten tribes of the north were destroyed by the invading Assyrians and in 586 BCE, the two southern tribes were taken into exile in Babylon. Nonetheless, they retained their faith and in 538 King Cyrus of Persia allowed them to return and rebuild the Temple in Jerusalem. The Temple was destroyed a second time in the first century CE by the Romans and all that remained was the Western Wall. The Jewish people were scattered over the face of the earth, but their sense of nationhood remained. They continued to pray in Hebrew; through their annual reading of the Pentateuch, they reminded themselves that God's promise was for all time; every year on the fast day of Av they mourned the loss of the Temple; every day in the synagogue they prayed that God would return to Jerusalem to reside there and 'build it soon ... as an eternal building'[1] and in the liturgical grace after meals they entreated God to raise up Jerusalem, the holy city, 'in our days'.

Perhaps most poignant of all was the spring festival of Passover. This is traditionally celebrated at home. Every year the extended family would gather together to celebrate their liberation from slavery in Egypt. The story of Moses was told once more; a large meal was eaten; songs were sung and family fellowship was enjoyed. At the conclusion of the evening, the head of the family would say solemnly to the assembled company: '*L'shanah haba'ah b'Yerushalayim*' − Next year, in Jerusalem!

The Zionist dream

Perfect in beauty, how in thee do love and grace unite!
    The souls of thy companions turn to thee; thy joy was their
        delight,
And weeping they lament thy ruin now. In exile, for thy height
    They long and to thy gates in prayer they bow ...[2]

So wrote the philosopher/poet Judah Halevi in the twelfth century of the city of Jerusalem. The modern Zionist movement grew out of this history of longing. Theodor Herzl (1860–1904), its founder, was a visionary in that he perceived that the return to the Promised Land could be achieved not by waiting for God to intervene directly in world history, but through the secular political process.

Herzl was a journalist. Initially he had believed that anti-Semitism, hatred of the Jews, would disappear when the Jewish people assimilated into the majority culture. He changed his mind as a result of the Dreyfus trial. Alfred Dreyfus (1859–1935) was a high-ranking French army officer and also a Jew. In 1894 he was accused of high treason and, although he consistently protested his innocence, he was sentenced to life imprisonment. It was subsequently discovered that the documents upon which his conviction was based had been forged, but nonetheless, when he was tried again in 1899, he was again found guilty. The affair caused a sensation. Many were convinced that Dreyfus was part of a Jewish plot designed to undermine the stability of France. He was eventually pardoned by the French president, but he was not formally exonerated of the crime until 1906. The whole episode made a huge impression on Herzl. As he himself put it: 'I became a Zionist because of the Dreyfus trial which I attended in 1894 ... the wild screams of the street mob near the building of the military school where it was ordered that Dreyfus be deprived of his rank still resounds in my ears.'[3]

Herzl argued that anti-Semitism would only cease being a problem if the Jewish people had a land of their own. To this end, he convened the First Zionist Congress in Basle in 1897 and he founded the World Zionist Organization, of which he was the first president. The annual congress served as the supreme legislative forum of the organization and attracted delegates from many countries. Herzl himself was interested first and foremost in establishing a Jewish homeland – he did not insist that the homeland should be in the traditional Promised Land. So at various times, part of Turkey, Cyprus, the Sinai peninsula and even an area of Uganda were considered. In fact the British approved this last suggestion, but it aroused such a storm of protest at the Sixth Zionist Congress that Herzl was compelled to affirm his commitment to Palestine as the only possible site. It is likely that this controversy was partly responsible for his premature death in 1904.

The old joke about four Jews and six opinions was never so true as in the Zionist movement. After Herzl's death, many Russian delegates, who were suffering pogroms and extensive civil disabilities, demanded the immediate beginning of effective colonization. This was known as 'practical Zionism'. A wave of immigrants departed for the Promised Land, most of whom were determined to earn their living by farming. Many combined Jewish nationalism with Marxist convictions and they were determined to create an international Hebrew, rather than an Eastern European Yiddish, culture. On the other side there were the 'political Zionists' who shared Herzl's conviction that diplomatic activity was the way to achieve a Jewish state. Their greatest achievement was the Balfour Declaration. This was a British statement of sympathy with Zionist aspirations signed by the British foreign secretary, Lord Balfour, in 1917.

There were religious differences as well. Many of the Western European delegates were only concerned with the political needs of the Jewish people and they ignored all religious aspects. In response Rabbi Isaac Reines (1839–1915) formed the Mizrachi party, the Strictly Orthodox wing of the Zionist movement. Mizrachi stated its aim as the 'perpetuation of the Jewish people in the observance of Torah ... and the return to the land of our forefathers'. There was constant conflict between the religious and secular Zionists, particularly in educational and cultural matters. At the same time, there were differences between those who emphasized Zionism as an expression of Jewish civilization and those who insisted that the role of Zionism was to create a socialist state based on the biblical concept of justice. Then there were others who rejected the Zionist dream altogether ...

The anti-Zionists

Opposition to Zionism came from the two extreme wings of the religious spectrum. On the one hand, the nineteenth-century Reformers saw assimilation, not the creation of a Jewish homeland, as the solution to anti-Semitism. Reform Jews had consistently stressed the universal message of Judaism. They understood the Jewish heritage as a call to ethical monotheism. In the words of the biblical prophet Micah, the Jew was 'to do justice, to love mercy and to walk humbly with thy God' (6:8). The mission of Judaism was to bring the knowledge of the One God and His ethical will to the nations of the world. They were uneasy with the particularistic elements of the tradition and they had already abandoned prayers for the restoration of the sacrificial system in the Temple in Jerusalem.

After Herzl issued his summons to the First Zionist Congress, the Progressive German rabbis made a statement declaring that the Jewish faith obligated all Jews to serve the countries in which they live. The American Reformers were even more downright. Isaac Mayer Wise (1819–1900), the first president of the American Reform rabbinical college, declared: 'We denounce the whole question of the Jewish State as foreign to the spirit of the modern Jew of this land, who looks upon America as his Palestine and whose interests are centred here.'[4] These early Reformers believed that the salvation of the Jews lay not in the return to the Promised Land, but in the emergence of a liberal, educated and pluralistic society.

Many members of the American Reform movement persisted in their opposition to Zionism right up until World War II. As late as 1942, a number of American anti-Zionists gathered together to formulate a programme of action. This body asserted that the political aspirations of the Zionists were contrary to the universalistic spirit of Judaism and that Zionism threatened Jewry in that it called into question the loyalty of the

Jews to the countries in which they lived. Even after World War II, the American Reform liturgy for the Passover meal ended not with 'Next Year in Jerusalem', but with 'God bless America!'

Reform Jews therefore objected to Zionism because it undermined Jewish allegiance to host nations and because it emphasized the ethnic, nationalistic spirit of Judaism. Many of the Strictly Orthodox disapproved of Zionism for completely different reasons. Although the Torah teaches that it is the duty of all pious Jews to pray for the return to Zion, this ingathering must be preceded by the messianic redemption. Only when God has sent His long-promised 'anointed one' will the exiles of Israel return to the Holy Land and all nations will turn to Jerusalem to learn of the One God. The neo-Orthodox leader, Samson Raphael Hirsch (1808–88), had taught that it was forbidden to accelerate divine deliverance and that it would happen in God's good time. The Zionist movement was thus perceived as an evil conspiracy against God's will and yet another episode in the long history of false messianic hopes.

In 1912, a group of Strictly Orthodox Jews founded the Agudat Israel to preserve Torah Judaism. This organization was determined in its opposition to Zionism, which they saw as a threat to Orthodoxy. As Rabbi Shalom Dov Schneersohn (1866–1920) put it, the Zionists 'make the impression ... that the whole purpose of Torah ... is merely to strengthen collective feeling. This theory can easily be adopted by young people who regard themselves as instruments prepared for the fulfilment of the Zionist ideal. They naturally regard themselves as completely liberated from the Torah and the commandments for now, they think, nationalism has replaced religion, and is the best means for the preservation of society.'[5]

Nonetheless, the Orthodox anti-Zionists did accept that it was desirable to return to the Promised Land, and among the early settlers there was a strong Orthodox presence. In the early days, its leaders used to campaign against the Zionists, protesting to the British government and the League of Nations about their nationalistic aspirations. On occasions they even joined forces with the Arab leaders who were disturbed by the increased Jewish presence in Palestine. So deep was the rift between the Zionists and the ultra-Orthodox that a member of the Agudat Israel executive was assassinated by the Jewish underground military organization in 1924. In response, one Orthodox spokesman declared that the Zionists were 'evil men and ruffians' and that Hell had entered Israel with Theodor Herzl.

The Jewish state

The Holocaust changed everything. After World War I, anti-Semitism was rife even in such traditionally tolerant countries as Great Britain and the United States. Accusations against the Jews were frequently contradictory. On the one hand, they were said to exert undue influence over the commercial life of the capitalist world; on the other, it was thought that they were fomenting revolution and were the cause of the rise of communism. Adolf Hitler (1889–1945), who became chancellor of Germany in 1933, made no secret of his hatred. He argued that the Jews were degenerates and parasites, that Germany had lost the war because of the treachery of Jewish socialists, liberals and pacifists and he insisted that the Russian revolution of 1917 had been part of a world-wide Jewish conspiracy.

Once the Nazis had invaded Poland in 1939 there was no escape for the Jews living in Germany and occupied Europe. Initially the Nazi ruling powers dealt with the Jewish population by what they euphemistically described as 'destruction through work'. This was not effective enough and in 1942 the decision was made to annihilate the Jews systematically in a network of concentration and extermination camps. The figures speak for themselves. In 1939 world Jewry numbered approximately sixteen-and-a-half million people. By the end of World War II, it had been reduced by six million. The historic Jewish communities of Eastern Europe had been totally destroyed in the death camps of Auschwitz, Belzec, Majdanek, Sobibor, Treblinka and Chelmno.

All too often the pathetic survivors of the concentration camps found that they were not welcome when they tried to return to their old homes. Their gentile neighbours had taken possession of their property and had no intention of returning it. In Poland several Holocaust survivors were murdered. In a very real sense these people were homeless and had no alternative but to wait in displaced persons' camps while the international community tried to decide what was to be done with them. Meanwhile the British had held Palestine since World War I. Despite the Balfour Declaration, they were restricting Jewish immigration in an attempt to keep the peace between the Jewish and Arab populations. By 1947 they had had enough. They handed over the whole problem to the United Nations.

On 29 November 1947, the General Assembly endorsed the suggestion that there be separate Arab and Jewish states in the area. The Arabs were bitterly opposed to this solution and immediately began attacking Jewish settlements. Although they had a far larger army than the Jews, the Jewish leaders succeeded in consolidating their holdings. On 14 May 1948 they formally declared the independence of the new State of Israel. According to the Scroll of Independence, the new nation existed 'by virtue of our national and intrinsic right and on the strength of the resolution of the United Nations General Assembly'.

The horror of the Holocaust and the creation of the State of Israel effectively ended any serious opposition to Zionism in the Reform community. It was generally recognized that the early Reform leaders had been misguided in their opposition to the creation of a Jewish homeland. The study of Hebrew and Israeli culture has become a central element in the curriculum of Reform religion schools. Reform congregations have become generous contributors to Israeli causes. Reform institutions have been established, despite Orthodox opposition, in the Jewish state and for many Reform Jews, the State of Israel has become pivotal in their understanding of Judaism and the Jewish people. In 1976 the movement produced the San Francisco Platform, a declaration of the beliefs of American Reform Judaism. In this it is maintained: 'We are privileged to live in an extraordinary time, one in which a third Jewish commonwealth has been established in our people's ancient homeland. We are bound to that land and to the newly reborn State of Israel. We have both a stake and a responsibility in building the State of Israel.'[6]

The ultra-Orthodox capitulation to Zionism has not been quite so complete. The traditionally anti-Zionist Agudat Israel party has come to terms with the Jewish state and now participates in its national life. Nonetheless the more extreme Orthodox elements still refuse to accept the legitimacy of the State of Israel. Some go so far as to live in the Holy Land, perhaps in Mea Shearim in Jerusalem or in Bene Beraknear Tel Aviv, but they take no part in the political process. They continue to believe that only the Messiah can re-establish a Jewish commonwealth on earth. As they have done for centuries, they will wait and pray for his coming.

Israel and Jewish identity

The murder of six million in the Holocaust and the creation of the modern State of Israel have had profound repercussions for the Jewish community. As was indicated in Chapter 1, the Holocaust raises the most acute theological problem, how it is possible to believe in an all-powerful, all-knowing and all-loving God when one-third of world Jewry was systematically destroyed in the most appalling conditions. In the days of Moses, God is said to have rescued His people from slavery in Egypt. Yet in the mid-twentieth century, countless cattle trucks crowded with Jews rattled their way across central Europe. Their destination was the gas chambers of Auschwitz, but the Heavens remained silent. God did not intervene.

Insofar as any sense at all can be made of the Holocaust, for many Jews the imperative that has emerged is that of survival. In the words of the Canadian theologian Emil Fackenheim (1916–2003): 'Jews ... are commanded to survive as Jews lest the Jewish people perish. They are commanded to remember the victims of Auschwitz lest their memories perish.' He goes on to argue: 'They are forbidden to despair of the God of Israel, lest Judaism perish,' but this part of his message is apt to be forgotten.[7] The Jewish community has concentrated on keeping the Holocaust memory alive with or without God. There is a proliferation of Holocaust memorials, museums and commemoration projects. Auschwitz itself has become a place of pilgrimage and a Jewish shrine. In fact, many people who were not Jews died in Hitler's concentration camps, but when a Christian convent was set up at Auschwitz so that nuns could pray for the souls of the victims, the Jewish community was outraged. It was seen as a Christian invasion and appropriation of a Jewish sacred site. The Holocaust has become an essential part of modern Jewish self-understanding. In a very real sense the community has taken to heart Fackenheim's dictum, 'You must not grant Hitler a posthumous victory.'[8]

The State of Israel has provided the second new focus for Jewish identity and again, for many Jews, this is a secular rather than a religious loyalty. For centuries Jews have prayed for their return to the Holy Land. This would be part of God's redemption of the world. Some time in the future, God would send His Anointed One, His Messiah, who would establish peace on earth and who would gather together again the scattered remnants of Israel. Theodor Herzl's Zionism, on the other hand, was of a very different order. The Jews would return to the land of their forefathers not because of divine intervention, but as a result of determined political lobbying and diplomacy. Admittedly some religious Zionists have tried to understand the establishment of the State of Israel as the beginning of the prophetic redemption. But, with the best will in the world, it is hard to reconcile the political events in modern Israel with the great messianic vision of the prophet Isaiah: 'The wolf shall dwell with the lamb, and the leopard shall lie down with the kid, and the calf and the lion and the fatling together, and a little child shall lead them ... They shall not hurt or destroy in all my holy mountain ... for the earth shall be full of the knowledge of the Lord as the waters cover the sea' (11:6, 9).

For many, the State of Israel is the only consolation for the Holocaust. It has become a metaphor for renewal and hope. The Jewish state is seen as the guarantee that a similar calamity can never again befall the Jewish people. To that end the Israeli Law of Return offers citizenship to Jews living anywhere in the world. In any country, whether persecution threatens or not, a Jew can go to the Israeli embassy, register as an Israeli citizen and find new life and security in the Promised Land. Immediately then, the problem arises as to who is to be counted as a Jew. Many people who suffered as Jews in Hitler's Germany would not be counted as such by the Strictly Orthodox – perhaps they had only one Jewish grandparent. Similarly in the countries of the former Soviet Union, those whom officialdom registers as Jews may well have a Jewish father but not a Jewish mother. It is highly unlikely that the black Jewish community of Ethiopia is physically descended from the ancient Israelites and even less probable that they underwent Orthodox conversions. Yet these people perceive themselves as Jews and have suffered as a result of this perception. In consequence the State of Israel has broadened its definition of Jewishness away from the strictly religious boundaries, so that all these refugees can be accommodated. At the end of the day, Israel is a political rather than a religious reality.

Thus in the Jewish community we find many whose attachment to Judaism is essentially secular. They no longer believe in a loving God who guides His Chosen People through the vicissitudes of history. Instead thay feel a strong determination to survive as a nation. They keep the memory of the Holocaust alive and they are intensely loyal and generous in their concern for the State of Israel. Today there are many Jews whose main connection with Jewish life is their regular donation to Israeli projects and charities. They may not be religious, but they do support Israel.

5
The future hope

The Messiah

Through the long centuries of exile from the Promised Land, the Jewish people did not wait and pray for the creation of a secular Jewish state. The idea would have been incomprehensible. Certainly they expected that one day they would return to the land, since it had been given to them as an everlasting possession. But the return would be accompanied by a series of long-promised signs that God Himself was about to intervene in the history of the world. Central to these expectations would be the advent of the longed-for king, the Messiah.

Belief in the coming of the Messiah was the twelfth of Moses Maimonides' (1135–1204) Thirteen Principles of the Jewish Faith:

> We should believe and affirm that the Messiah will come ... No date may be fixed for his appearance, nor may the Scriptures be interpreted in such a way as to derive from them the time of his coming ... We should have firm faith in him, honouring and loving him and praying for his coming in accordance with what has been said about him by all the prophets from Moses to Malachi. Whoever has doubts about him or makes light of his authority, contradicts the Torah ... A consequence of this principle is that Israel cannot have a king who is not descended from David.[1]

The conviction that the Messiah would be descended from the biblical King David (eleventh/tenth century BCE) goes back to the account of the election and anointing of David. God was said to have chosen David and his descendants to rule over Israel until the end of time. After the collapse of David's empire, this promise was understood as a prophecy of the future and gradually there grew up a mythology around this future monarch. He would establish truth and justice and his reign would last forever. Through the centuries, the idea of this future Messiah grew and developed. By the time that the Romans were occupying the land in the first century BCE, it was understood that he would redeem and rule the people at the climax of human history and he would be the instrument by which God's kingdom would be established on earth.

There have been many messianic claimants. The New Testament mentions one Theudas who 'gave himself out to be somebody' and Judas the Galilean who 'drew away some of the people after him' (Acts 5:36–7). According to the first-century historian Josephus, Judas's son, Menahem, was killed in the Temple after he had dressed himself in royal robes. Jesus was perceived by his followers as the Messiah – the title Christ is the Greek translation of the Hebrew Messiah. He was rejected by the majority of the Jewish people because he failed to bring about the glorious events associated with the messianic age. His followers were aware of this criticism and responded to it by promising that in the near future he would return again; the world would see the 'Son of Man coming in clouds with great power and glory. And then he will send his angels and gather his elect from the four winds, from the ends of the earth to the ends of heaven' (Mark 13:26, 27).

Messianic claims did not stop with Jesus. In the second century CE, Simeon bar Kokhba led a rebellion against the Romans and was recognized as the Messiah by Rabbi Akiva, the most famous legal authority of the day. Bar Kokhba was killed in battle while Akiva was eventually flayed alive by the Romans. Several small messianic movements occurred between the seventh and ninth centuries. A miracle-working Messiah had appeared either in Lyons, France or Leon, Spain, in 1060. There were further messianic candidates in the twelfth century. The most prominent of these was David Alroy who led the Jews of Baghdad to believe that they would all fly to Jerusalem on the wings of angels. More serious were the claims of Shabbetai Zevi (1626–76) who was expected to depose the Turkish sultan and take over his earthly rule. The whole Jewish world was in a ferment and the excitement only died down when Shabbetai was arrested in Constantinople. He was given the choice between death and conversion to Islam and, to the great scandal of the community, he chose the latter alternative.

Even today some sectors have been carried away by messianic fervour. A possible candidate appeared in the shape of Menahem Mendel Schneersohn (1902–94), the last leader of the Lubavitcher Hasidim. Even after his death, some of his follow-ers remain convinced that he will return again. The majority of the Strictly Orthodox, however, are content to wait and pray for some future figure. Meanwhile, the rest of the Jewish world is increasingly looking to other forms of salvation.

The messianic age

One traditional element in the belief in the coming of the Messiah is that he will bring in a golden age. This desirable state of affairs is described by several of the biblical prophets, includ-ing Ezekiel:

> I will take the people of Israel from the nations among whom they have gone and will gather them from all sides, and bring them to their own land ... They shall not defile themselves any more with idols ... and they shall be My people and I will be their God. My servant David shall be king over them ... I will make a covenant of peace with them ... My dwelling place shall

be with them; and I will be their God and they shall be My
people. (37:23–7)

The rabbis interpreted these words to mean that the king-
Messiah would bring in a time of unsullied human happiness. He
would initiate peace in the world and he would promote justice
and teach Torah. It must be remembered that the Messiah was
always understood as a human figure. So the true author of this
anticipated redemption is God Himself. It is He who will right
all wrongs and bring a state of healing to the earth; It is He who
will restore the twelve tribes to the Promised Land and will
establish His righteous kingdom for all time.

The modern Zionist movement despiritualized the promise
of the return to the land in their establishment of a national
Jewish state. Earlier and similarly, the Reform movement had
secularized the traditional concept of the messianic age. By the
nineteenth century, the Reform leaders no longer expected or
desired the setting up of a theocracy in the Promised Land. As
they put it in the Pittsburgh Platform of 1885: 'We consider
ourselves no longer a nation, but a religious community, and
therefore expect neither a return to Palestine, nor a sacrificial
worship under the sons of Aaron, nor the restoration of any of
the laws concerning the Jewish State.'[2] They also rejected the
idea of the Messiah as too particularistic and nationalistic. Instead
these early Reformers looked for a universalistic messianic age.
They believed that the whole world would become perfected
led by the example of Jewish monotheism. The nineteenth
century was a period of great intellectual optimism; huge
advances were being made in terms of scientific knowledge and
social, economic and educational reforms. These measures were
heralded as the foretaste of the messianic era. Again quoting
from the Pittsburgh Platform, the Reform leaders declared: 'We
recognize in the modern era of universal culture of heart and
intellect the approaching of the realization of Israel's great

messianic hope for the establishment of the kingdom of truth, justice and peace among all men.'

This optimism was sadly dashed by the carnage of World War I and by the renewed anti-Semitism of the Depression years. Nonetheless the Reform rabbis continued to stress the human obligation to bring about a divine kingdom on earth:

> Throughout the ages it has been Israel's mission to witness to the Divine in the face of easy paganism and materialism. We regard it as our historic task to cooperate with all men in the establishment of the kingdom of God, of universal brotherhood, justice, truth and peace on earth. This is our messianic goal.[3]

The catastrophe of the Holocaust converted the last doubters in the Reform camp to the desirability of the Zionist dream. At the same time, the Reform movement remained committed to social action as the human means of bringing in the messianic age. In the mid-twentieth century, Reform Jews were in the forefront of the civil rights demonstrations and they were prominent in the women's liberation campaigns and in the various peace movements. Even today non-Orthodox Jews tend to be liberal in their political opinions and positive in their attitude to all forms of social reform. There are many synagogues, particularly in the United States, which are nationally known for their dedication to and support of social action projects. Indeed, it is a frequent complaint of many Reform Jews that they would like to hear more about spirituality from the pulpit and less about political campaigns!

So just as the old doctrine of the divine ingathering of the exiles by the Messiah has been transmuted into support for the national state of Israel, so has the traditional expectation of God establishing His kingdom on earth been transformed for many Jews into a secular commitment to social, political and educational reform. It is not surprising that the leaders of many of today's most radical movements are Jewish in origin. As the twentieth-century philosopher Martin Buber (1878–1965) expressed it: 'Israel can never turn away its face from the state ... at the same time it must long for the perfection of the state ... Both the conservative and the revolutionary Jewish attitudes stem from the same [messianic feelings].'[4]

Immortality

Besides looking for the return to the Promised Land and a future golden age, many Jews also retain a hope in personal immortality. This belief arose relatively late in the history of Judaism. There are few references to life after death in the Hebrew scriptures. A number of expressions are employed to signify the realm of the dead. In Psalm 88, for example, the writer complains, 'My soul is full of troubles, and my life draws near to Sheol. I am reckoned among those who go down to the Pit; I am a man who has no strength, like one forsaken among the dead, like the slain that lie in the grave, like those whom Thou dost remember no more' (3–5). The implication is that after death, a human being is discarded and is forgotten even by God Himself. Sheol, the place of the dead, seems to have been perceived as a shadowy region where the dead have no substance. In Psalm 6, the poet declares: 'For in death there is no remembrance of Thee; in Sheol, who can give Thee praise?' (5).

Later, however, a doctrine of immortality developed. Possibly as a result of Persian influence during and after the exile in Babylon (in the sixth century BCE), it was thought that the bodies of the dead would be resurrected. There are two references to this in the Bible, both considered by biblical scholars to be of a late date. In the book of Isaiah, it is said, 'The dead shall live, their bodies shall rise. O dwellers in the dust, awake and sing for joy' (26:19) and, according to the book of Daniel,

'Many of those who sleep in the dust of the earth shall awake' (12:2). This belief was connected with the doctrine of the Messiah. After the Jewish people had been restored to the Holy Land in the messianic age, then the dead would be resurrected from their graves.

In the years before the destruction of Jerusalem in CE 70, there was conflict over the doctrine. On the one hand the Sadducees, the aristocratic priestly caste, rejected it as unbiblical. On the other, the Pharisees, the teachers of the law, accepted it and argued that it was implicit in the scriptural text. So, for example, Rabbi Eleazar maintained that the verse in the book of Numbers 'that person shall be utterly cut off, his iniquity shall be upon him' (15:31) only makes sense if the sinner is cut off in this life and then held responsible for his iniquity in the next. It was part of the Pharisaic world view that after the dead had been resurrected, the final judgement would take place.

The twelfth-century philosopher Maimonides listed belief in the resurrection as the last of his Principles of the Jewish Faith, but, in fact, he wrote little about it. The rabbis of the Talmud clearly believed in a straightforward physical resurrection, since the dead are described as rising wearing their clothes. Maimonides was uneasy with this idea. In his *Essay on Resurrection*, he went so far as to argue that even though the dead would come to life again, like all physical entities, they would die again in the course of time. He believed that only the souls of human beings are truly immortal.

Today, most Jews who believe in any form of life after death would agree with him. The old doctrine of the resurrection of the body was so closely tied in with that of the Messiah that once the messianic concept faded into the background, so also did the resurrection. A physical rising seems almost inconceivable in the light of a modern, scientific understanding of the world. Both the Orthodox and the Reform communities prefer to stress the idea of the immortality of the soul. So, for example, the late Chief Rabbi of the British Commonwealth, Dr J. H. Hertz, insisted that 'Many and various are the folk beliefs and poetical fancies ... but our most authoritative religious guides, however, proclaim that no eye has seen, nor can mortal fathom, what awaiteth us in the Hereafter; but that even the tarnished soul will not forever be denied spiritual bliss.'[5] In the Reform camp, Rabbi Gunther Plaut has written: 'Reform Jews reassert the doctrine of Judaism that the soul is immortal ... We reject as ideas not rooted in Judaism the belief in bodily resurrection.'[6] Thus it seems that today the Jewish belief in the immortality of the soul has been disassociated from the traditional notion of the messianic redemption and also, it will appear, from ideas of reward and punishment.

Reward and punishment

Belief in reward and punishment is the logical corollary of belief in an all-powerful, all-just God. It is a matter of common experience in this life that all too often the virtuous suffer and the wicked prosper. God's justice can only be served if there is another life in which this balance is redressed. It is only fair that the good should receive their reward and that the bad should have cause to regret their misdeeds. Since this does not happen in this life, then clearly it must be a feature of the world to come. As the rabbis of the Talmud put it, 'The world is a place where the commandments are obeyed; the world to come is the place of reward for keeping them.'[7]

According to Maimonides: 'The eleventh fundamental Principle [of the Jewish Faith] is that God rewards him who obeys the commands of the Torah and punishes him who transgresses its prohibitions. The greatest of God's rewards is the world to come, and the severest of His punishments is cutting off.'[8] The whole doctrine of reward and punishment, as well as that of the messianic age and the resurrection of the dead, developed after the exile in Babylon in the sixth century BCE. It is not found in the Hebrew scriptures. The rabbis of the Second Temple period and of the first centuries of the Common Era produced no systematic statement of belief on the subject. The general pattern seems to have been that during the messianic age there would be a general resurrection of the dead and this would be followed by a final judgement. There was also, confusingly, the idea that the individual soul would be judged after death, but the relationship between this judgement and the general resurrection is not clear.

It was agreed, however, that the righteous would enter Heaven (or the Garden of Eden). This was portrayed in different ways in the literature. One of the earliest descriptions is found in Midrash Konen:

> There are five chambers for the various classes of the righteous. The first is ... the habitation of non-Jews who become true and devoted converts to Judaism ... The second is ... the habitation of the penitents. The third chamber ... contains the best of heaven and earth ... The fourth chamber is inhabited by those who have suffered for the sake of their religion ... The fifth chamber is built of precious stones and ... is inhabited by the Messiah of David, Elijah and the Messiah of Ephraim.[9]

Conversely, the wicked are subjected to dreadful torture: 'Some sinners were suspended by their eyelids, some by their ears, some by their hands and some by their tongues ... These sinners were punished in this way because they swore falsely, profaned the Sabbath and the Holy Days, despised the sages, called their neighbours by unseemly nicknames, wronged the orphan and the widow and bore false witness.'[10] All these doctrines were expressed in the narrative sections of rabbinic literature; unlike the law, they were not binding and this meant that there was room for considerable difference of opinion in these matters.

In the modern era, the Jewish community has largely abandoned these beliefs. It is interesting that when faced with the enormity of the Holocaust, in general Jewish theologians have not turned to these traditional doctrines to find some sort of explanation for God's silence. If the innocent victims of the concentration camps are not compensated for their sufferings in the world to come, then there is no ultimate justice. Yet this avenue has scarcely been explored. In his commentary on the traditional Prayer Book, Chief Rabbi Hertz categorically asserted that 'Judaism rejects the doctrine of eternal punishment.' Similarly the Reform theologian Kaufmann Kohler argued: 'Our modern conception of time and space admit neither a place or a world-period for the reward and punishment of souls, nor the intolerable conception of eternal joy without useful action and eternal agony without any moral purpose.'[11]

Thus traditional rabbinic eschatology has lost its force for a large number of Jews in the modern period. This is no small omission. In the past, the belief in reward and punishment helped the pious Jew make sense of the world as the creation of a just and loving God. He could be confident that he would be compensated for his sufferings in this life in the hereafter. Without this conviction, it seems impossible to reconcile the idea of a God who cares for His Chosen People with the cataclysmic events of the Holocaust. It is hard to see how, without such a belief, it is possible to retain any hope for the righteous of Israel.

Survival

So what is the Jewish hope for the future? The Strictly Orthodox continue to wait for God's anointed, His Messiah, who will bring in the messianic age. The scattered remnants of the Jewish people will be gathered in from the four corners of the earth and will return to Jerusalem. Ultimately the dead will be resurrected and a final judgement will ensue. Then, in the world to come, the righteous will enjoy a life of bliss while the wicked will receive their just deserts. As the Italian mystic Moses Luzzatto (1707–47) put it:

> Our sages of blessed memory have taught us that man was created to find delight in the Lord and to bask in the radiance of His presence, for this is true happiness and the greatest of all possible delight ... This world is like a vestibule before the world to come ... Man is put here in order to earn the place which has been prepared for him in the world-to-come.[12]

Yet today the Strictly Orthodox are a small minority of the Jewish people. For the rest, the answer is less straightforward. The non-Orthodox movements have retained the doctrines of the messianic age and the immortality of the soul, but the messianic age will come about through human endeavour and the soul does not have to confront the possibility of eternal torment. It is a bloodless scenario compared with the robust convictions that sustained the Jewish community in the past. Very many other Jews go still further. They no longer expect any form of messianic redemption; they do not anticipate that God will ever make His presence known in the world and they have lost all belief in personal immortality. In short, they have regained the biblical idea that as far as human consciousness goes, this world is all that there is. At the same time they have lost the crucial biblical sense of God being an agent in human history in the here and now.

If keeping the commandments is no longer seen as a prepa-ration for eternity, then what is the point of the continued existence of Judaism? This problem does exercise the non-Orthodox community. For many, the answer lies in the State of Israel. The founding of the Jewish state has become the central focus of their religious and cultural identity. Throughout the world, Jews have a deep admiration for the astonishing achievements of the Israelis in reclaiming the desert and in building a new society. They follow Middle Eastern affairs closely; they give lavishly to Israeli causes and they think seriously of emigrating themselves. For such people, Judaism has become Zionism and Jewishness is a national rather than a religious identity.

For others, Jewish survival has become an end in itself. Hitler succeeded in murdering a third of world Jewry. It has become a matter of principle that he should not, over fifty years after his death, succeed in finishing the job. Those who hold this view may, in fact, do nothing Jewish. They may have no inclination to belong to a synagogue; they may prefer that their children attend non-Jewish schools; they may participate in no Jewish projects and they may consciously avoid living in a Jewish area. Nonetheless, if one of their children announces that they have fallen in love with a non-Jewish person, an explosion ensues. The erring offspring is told that he or she is betraying the Jewish people, is aiding Hitler's work and is dishonouring the memory of the innocent victims of the Holocaust. Perhaps not surprisingly by that stage, the children take little notice. In many countries outside Israel, the out-marriage rate for Jewish young people is more than 50 per cent.

Both the Orthodox and the non-Orthodox establishment are acutely aware of the problem. They know that the twin pillars of support for the State of Israel and horror at the remembrance of the Holocaust will not be enough to sustain religious Jewish identity through the next millennium. As yet they have not succeeded in stemming the rising tide of secularism and indifference. Nonetheless the Jewish religion, even in its less traditional manifestations, continues to speak to many people. As one dedicated member of the community put it in conversation with the authors:

Jewish continuity for me is the whole thing really. Why? That's a good question. Why? There's always the argument that says you give Hitler the posthumous victory, but I'm not one that says we have to survive because Hitler said we shouldn't. I think there's inherent value in what Judaism has to offer to ourselves and the world ... I think we have a great set of values, wonderful celebrations, great ethics ... There's a wonderful tradition of study and I think it can enrich anyone's life who really digs into it in a meaningful way ... I know it has done so for me personally.

6

Judaism and other religions

The one true God

In the modern era, there has been very little concern among Jewish theologians about other religions. Though, particularly since the Holocaust, there is an interest in the development of Jewish–Christian dialogue as well as in isolated instances of Jewish–Muslim encounter, the majority of Jewish writers have not seriously considered the place of Judaism in the context of the religious experience of humanity. This has not always been the case. From its earliest history, the Jews were compelled to encounter idolatry – the worship of many gods. Since the destruction of the Second Temple in CE 70, Jews have lived as a minority group among either a Christian or a Muslim population. In the ancient world and in the Middle Ages, Jews did come to certain conclusions about other religions.

The primary creed of the Jewish faith is 'Hear O Israel, the Lord our God, the Lord is One.' The very first of the Ten Commandments insists, 'You shall have no other gods before Me.' This is followed by the injunction, 'You shall not make for yourself a graven image ... You shall not bow down to them or serve them, for I the Lord your God am a jealous God' (Exodus 20:3–4). There were repeated warnings against the Canaanite religion. When the Jews entered the Promised Land, they were warned against consorting with original inhabitants: 'You shall make no covenant with them or with their gods. They shall not dwell in your land, lest they make you sin against Me; for if you serve other gods, it will surely be a snare to you' (Exodus 23:32–3). Most particularly Jewish men were warned against marrying outside their own people and, once an independent Jewish kingdom was established, the downfall of King Solomon was attributed to the idolatrous practices of his many foreign wives who 'turned his heart' (1 Kings 11:4).

The biblical historians judged all the Israelite kings by their faithfulness to God and by their acceptance or rejection of Canaanite elements in Jewish worship. So, for example, King Ahab was said to have done 'evil in the sight of the Lord more than all that were before him' (1 Kings 15:30). He was led astray by his wife Jezebel, the daughter of the powerful king of Phoenicia. When she married, she brought her own religious establishment with her and this included 450 prophets of the god Baal. It was these that the great Israelite prophet Elijah (ninth century BCE) challenged to a contest on Mount Carmel. There each party prepared sacrifices and prayed that their own god would send down fire from heaven. All day the prophets of Baal beseeched and cavorted, but nothing happened. When Elijah's turn came, however, 'the fire of the Lord fell and consumed the burnt offering and the wood and the stones and the dust and licked up the water that was in the trench. And when all the people saw it, they fell on their faces and they said: The Lord, He is God; the Lord, He is God' (1 Kings 18:38–9).

Thus it is clear that in biblical times, the Jews believed that their God was a reality while the gods of the other nations were either impotent or non-existent. This conviction is echoed in the messianic promise that some day, in the golden future, all the peoples of the world would turn to Jerusalem to learn the ways of the Lord. The situation became more complicated with the advent of Christianity and Islam. Christianity grew out of Judaism. Jesus (first century CE), the Christian messiah, was himself a Jew. Christians claim to believe in and worship the One God – albeit the One God who is also a trinity. Islam is also based on the belief in the One God. Muhammad (c.570–632), the Islamic prophet, taught that the Jewish prophets who went before were also true prophets, although they were less enlightened than he. Neither Muslims nor Christians could be dismissed as straightforward idolators and Maimonides (1135–1204) went so far as to argue that both Christianity and Islam have a role to play in teaching humanity essential truths about God, which would eventually prepare the world for the coming of the Messiah.

The traditional attitude, then, of Judaism to the religions of the world is that Judaism is true and the other religions are false – though Christianity and Islam are less in error than the others. This raises the question of missionizing and conversion: if Judaism is the only true religion, then surely it is the duty of all pious Jews to advertise the fact. For complicated reasons, however, this is not the view of the mainstream Jewish establishment.

Traditional attitudes to conversion

There is evidence that at one stage in its history, Judaism was a missionary religion. The Bible contains the story of Ruth, a Moabite woman. She had been married to a Jewish man and, after his death, she insisted on returning with her mother-in-law to the Jewish homeland. She said, 'Wherever you go I will go, and where you lodge I will lodge; your people shall be my people and your God my God' (Ruth 1:16). Ruth subsequently married Boaz, a prosperous Jewish farmer, and was to become the great-grandmother of no less a person than the great King David.

Ruth's conversion is an interesting paradigm. She became a member of the Jewish people as well as a believer in their God. It was not merely a matter of sharing a particular conviction, it was also a matter of joining a nation. In ancient times, people who lived among the Jews as permanent settlers were described in Hebrew as *gerim*. The term came to mean both converts and sojourners. They joined the Jewish people, assimilated their customs and gradually came to be regarded as full members of the society. Then there was the category of those who were compelled to convert. During the Hasmonean period (second century BCE), the independent Jewish kingdom conquered neighbouring Idumea and forced its inhabitants to espouse Judaism. King Herod (d. 4 BCE), who rebuilt the Temple in Jerusalem, was of Idumean origin and thus descended from a convert.

At this period, it seems that many non-Jews rejected paganism. They could no longer believe in gods who quarrelled among themselves, who made love and war indiscriminately and who appeared to be nothing more than powerful human beings. They were attracted to Judaism and the belief in one God, and they were encouraged by the Jewish religious establishment. Jesus described how the leaders 'traverse land and sea to make a single proselyte' (Matthew 23:15). When the first-century Christian missionary Paul was spreading his message round the Mediterranean Sea, he invariably visited the local synagogue. There he preached to the Jews and to those who were known as 'God-fearers'. These seem to have been people sympathetic to and interested in Judaism, but who were not willing to undergo full conversion rites. It has been conjectured that the God-fearers were mainly men. Their wives had happily become Jews, but conversion for men involves circumcision as a sign of the covenant. Nonetheless their children (since they had Jewish mothers) were born Jews and were full members of the community.

The Talmud contains several positive references to converts. It was said that conversion was part of God's salvationist scheme: 'The Holy One, blessed be He, dispersed the people of Israel among the nations in order that they may acquire proselytes.' It was asserted that the convert is dearer to God than the Israelite since he has come of his own accord, while the Israelites are believers as a result of the miracles exhibited on Mount Sinai, and it was said that the person who oppresses the convert is as one who oppresses God. However, there was also the well-known saying attributed to Rabbi Helbo (third/fourth century CE) that 'proselytes are as harmful to Israel as a scab'. This view was to become the majority opinion.

Several factors contributed to this. Firstly, Jews living in Christian and Muslim lands suffered severe penalties if they attempted to make converts from other religions. It was commonly a capital crime. In addition, the Jewish community itself deeply resented any attempt by Christian missionaries to seduce members of their own community away from Judaism. In the history of Christian Europe, there were many attempts to convert the Jews, either by persuasion, or by bribes or even by the threat of torture and death. Not surprisingly, the Jews acquired a real horror of such tactics and argued among themselves that if they hated it when applied to their own community, so it must be wrong to attempt to convert others to Judaism.

There still remained a problem. If Judaism is the one true religion, then surely it must be a duty to save the world by persuading others of its truth. This conclusion was avoided by the saying of Rabbi Joshua (first/second century CE) in the Talmud that 'the righteous of all peoples have a share in the World to Come'. The community came to believe that any gentile, provided he or she kept a few basic laws, would be included in God's salvation. These laws were the seven rules given to Noah after the great flood. They must avoid idolatry, blasphemy, murder, forbidden sexual congress, robbery, injustice and cruelty. Thus, the argument went, it was far easier to be included in the world to come as a righteous gentile than as a

Jew who must keep all the 613 commandments. Conversion diminishes rather than enhances one's chance of salvation. In view of the attitude of the Christian and Jewish world to Jewish missionizing, it was an ingenious way of making a virtue out of a necessity.

Conversion today

Nonetheless, over the centuries a few people continued to be attracted to the Jewish religion and a definite ritual was established for receiving them into the fold. First of all, motives must be examined. As the sixteenth-century code of law, the *Shulhan Arukh*, states: 'When the would-be proselyte presents himself, he should be examined lest he be motivated to enter the congregation by hope of financial gain or social advantage or by fear. A man is examined lest his motive be to marry a Jewish woman and a woman is questioned lest she have similar desires towards some Jewish man.'[1] If the potential convert's motives are pure, then he or she is told of the heaviness of the yoke of the Torah and how difficult it is to keep all the commandments. If the candidate still persists then there is a period of instruction to be undergone.

Finally, if all goes well, the male convert is circumcized and, when the wound has completely healed, he undergoes total immersion in a ritual bath. Three learned and pious Jews stand by and instruct him in some of the easy and some of the difficult commandments. In the case of a woman, only immersion is required. She is accompanied to the ritual bath by Jewish women and the learned men stand outside the door giving the instructions. After this, the convert is a full member of the community in every respect. He or she is given a new Hebrew name and is described as Son or Daughter of Abraham (the first Jew and thus himself a convert). The community is expected to treat him or her as one born Jewish. It is wrong to remind converts of their origins or in any way embarrass them.

Until the nineteenth century, conversion to Judaism was rare in the modern world. However, once the civil disabilities of Jews were removed and members of the community mixed freely in the secular world, problems arose. When Jews began to attend secular universities and join the professions, it was inevitable that they would have contact with their gentile counterparts. Romantic attachments were formed and the question of marriage loomed. Jewish law is adamant that Jews may only marry other Jews. Therefore, for those who wanted to remain within the community, but who also wanted to marry a non-Jewish sweetheart, conversion was the only solution. It is a statistical fact that Jewish men have been more likely to 'marry out' than Jewish women, and for them the problem is particularly acute. Jewishness is passed down through the mother. If a Jewish man wanted to marry a gentile woman, but was determined to have Jewish children, then the fiancée had to convert.

The Orthodox have remained firm that desire for marriage is an inadequate reason for conversion. For those who are really determined, the religious establishment insists that the potential convert leads a totally Jewish life. This involves an extensive course of instruction and lodging for a lengthy period in a strictly Orthodox household. The process lasts at least two years, possibly more. It is a real test of the proselyte's persistence, stamina and commitment.

The non-Orthodox movements, however, are more accommodating. In contrast to the Orthodox, the Reform and Conservative leaders believe that non-Jewish fiancé(e)s should positively be encouraged to convert – since otherwise the new family is likely to be lost to Judaism. In 1892 the Reform rabbinate decreed that any rabbi, with the concurrence of two associates, could accept into the Jewish faith any 'honourable and intelligent person, without any initiating rite'. In recent years rituals have been reintroduced and today many Reform rabbis insist on both circumcision and immersion. Nonetheless, the period of preparation is shorter (commonly a year) and the whole atmosphere is far more welcoming.

Not surprisingly then, the vast majority of conversions have been through the non-Orthodox movements. Since no central register is kept, it is impossible to estimate the number of people who have joined the Jewish people through conversion, but in the United States the number is reckoned to be several hundred thousand. This raises an enormous problem. The Orthodox do not recognize non-Orthodox converts as Jews. Similarly, they perceive the children and grand-children of such female prose-lytes as gentiles. Thus, in the countries of the Dispersion, there are a growing number of people who believe themselves to be Jews, who identify with the community and who bring up their children as Jews, but who are not recognized as such by an important sector of their co-religionists. This is a time-bomb waiting to explode and arguably the essential unity of the Jewish people has been broken for ever.

Anti-Semitism

All too often the Jewish attitude to other religions has been forged in response to anti-Semitic prejudice. The term 'anti-Semitism' was first coined by the German journalist Wilhelm Marr (1818–1904) in the 1870s. He believed that German civilization was being systematically 'Judaized' and destroyed. This theme was taken up by many writers; for example, the journalist Otto Glagau wrote in the periodical *Die Gartenlaube*: 'Members of the Jewish tribe do not work. They exploit the mental and manual work of others. This alien tribe has enslaved the people of Germany. Basically the social question is the Jewish question.'

This was a new twist in the saga of Jewish hatred. Previously the Jews had been despised for their religious beliefs. The Christian Church saw itself as the New Israel and as the heir of the covenant. In their rejection of Jesus as the Messiah, Jews were thought to have disinherited themselves from God's favour. They had turned their backs on salvation – worse still, they had murdered God's Saviour. As a matter of fact, Jesus was killed by the Roman occupiers for political reasons. They understood that the term 'Messiah' meant 'king' and anyone who claimed to be a king was undermining the power of the mighty Roman empire. However, the Gospel writers, for reasons of expediency, preferred to stress the role of the Jews. Particularly in the gospel of Matthew, Jesus's crucifixion is presented as the result of Jewish pressure:

> Pilate [the Roman Governor] said to them [the Jews], 'Then what shall I do with Jesus who is called the Christ?' They all said, 'Let him be crucified' ... So when Pilate saw that he was gaining nothing, but rather that a riot was beginning, he took water and washed his hands before the crowd, saying, 'I am innocent of this man's blood. See to it yourselves.' And all the people answered, 'His blood be on us and on our children.'
> (27:22, 24–5)

For centuries, Jews were accused of being 'Christ-killers'; they had been rejected by God and they were damned everlastingly in consequence. Yet conversion to Christianity was always an option. Once a Jew abandoned his or her ancestral faith and was baptized, in general, persecution ceased. What was new in the anti-Semitism of Wilhelm Marr and his followers was that it was hatred of an ethnic group. However assimilated, however Christianized, the Jew was still regarded as an alien foreigner, a cancer in the nation. This kind of prejudice culminated in Hitler's destruction of the six million in the Holocaust. The

Nazi definition of Judaism had nothing to do with religion. A Jew was defined as anyone who had one Jewish grandparent. Jewish hatred was always expressed in racial terms. As Hitler himself put it: 'The black-haired youth lies in wait for hours on end. Satanically glaring at and spying on the unsuspicious girl whom he plans to seduce, adulterating her blood.'[2] Many of the Jews who died in the concentration camps had no religious beliefs. They were convicted out of hand for their genetic inheritance.

Anti-Semitism did not disappear with the Holocaust. Such tracts as *The Protocols of the Elders of Zion* are still circulated. The claim that Jews are organizing a conspiracy to take over the world still finds ready listeners among extreme right-wing groups in the West. The old communist states of Eastern Europe have long histories of Jew-hatred which are not easily abandoned, and anti-Semitic propaganda is seized upon in the Muslim countries where the inhabitants are still outraged by the creation of a Jewish state in their midst.

Nonetheless, the Holocaust has changed attitudes, not least because the Jews themselves are determined that it will never happen again. Countering anti-Semitism has become a positive industry. The Anti-Defamation League in the United States and the Institute of Jewish Affairs in Great Britain monitor all instances of anti-Jewish activity and urge constant vigilance on the community. Indeed, it could be argued that such carefulness goes too far. All too easily, any negative comment on the activities of the Israeli government, however well reasoned, is dismissed as yet another instance of prejudice. Gentiles who criticize the Jewish community are not invariably anti-Semitic, nor is their Jewish counterpart inevitably a 'self-hating' Jew. Judaism and Jewish civilization should not be solely rooted in countering anti-Semitism. Much remains to be done also in the promotion of positive Jewish values and in encouraging dialogue between the communities.

Dialogue

Despite the many centuries of Jew-hatred, there has been a concerted effort in recent years, particularly among Christians, to reach an understanding with Jews. In 1965, the Roman Catholic Church issued the decree *Nostra Aetate*. This recognized the spiritual bond that links Christians and Jews and affirmed God's continuing covenant: 'God holds the Jews most dear for the sake of their Fathers.' It went on to recommend fostering 'mutual understanding and respect which is the fruit, above all, of biblical and theological studies as well as fraternal dialogues'. Most importantly, it repudiated the ancient accusation of Christ-killing: 'True the Jewish authorities and those who followed their lead pressed for the death of Christ, still, what happened in his passion cannot be charged against all the Jews without distinction then alive, nor against the Jews of today.'[3]

Similar statements have been made by the World Council of Churches. Today the official line of that body is that the covenant of God with the Jewish world remains valid. All forms of anti-Semitism are to be repudiated. Coercive proselytism of the Jews is incompatible with Christianity and the living tradition of Judaism is a gift of God. On a more personal level, the Council of Christians and Jews was set up as a result of the events of World War II to foster mutual understanding between members of the two faiths. It sponsors meetings and lectures. Branches exist in most major cities in Europe and America.

Dialogue with the Muslim community has proved more difficult. The State of Israel has proved a huge stumbling block, and the Arab nations in particular still smart at the thought of its creation in their territory. The Jews, on their side, have not forgotten the resolution, sponsored by the Arab world and passed by the General Assembly of the United Nations, equating Zionism with racism. Relations between Blacks and Jews in the United States are not all they should be and this hostility is fanned by Black Muslim groups. The charismatic leader of the Nation of Islam, Malcolm X, used to argue, on very little historical evidence, that the Jews were largely responsible for the slave trade. His best-known successor, Louis Farrakhan, has had no hesitation in describing Hitler as a great man and Judaism as a 'gutter religion'.

Nonetheless, the horrific consequences of anti-Semitism have made an impression. Ordinary people can see all too clearly that the Holocaust was the result of uncontrolled Jew-hatred. They are anxious to enter into dialogue and learn more about the Jews, this mysterious group which has lived among them for so long. It must be said that the Jewish side does not always welcome such interest. The concern for Jewish survival is paramount. Many Jews are determined that their children do not become too involved in the gentile world, in case they are tempted to convert or marry out. The Strictly Orthodox, in particular, ask only to be allowed to live in peace in their own self-created communities. They have as little to do as possible with the non-Jewish world. *Yiddishkeit* (Jewish culture), as they call it, is best preserved by isolation.

Even relatively moderate Jews exact a high price for dialogue. In a recent lecture, the last Chief Rabbi of the British Commonwealth, Immanuel Jakobovits (1921–1999) informed his largely Christian audience that Christian–Jewish activities required certain preconditions. The Christian world must be whole-hearted in its support of the State of Israel; the churches must outlaw all missionary activity directed towards the Jews and they must understand that theological debate is not on the agenda (Lambeth Lecture, 1983). The Christian establishment is so guilt-ridden about the Holocaust and so anxious to be conciliatory that they largely go along with this. The 1996 policy document of the British Council of Christians and Jews declares that all 'aggressive missionizing' is wrong. When enquiries were made to the Council as to the precise meaning of this phrase, the present authors were told that any missionary activity directed against Jews was, by definition, aggressive. It seems that Jesus' final injunction to his followers to 'Go therefore and make disciples of all nations, baptizing them in the name of the Father and of the Son and of the Holy Ghost' is now interpreted to mean 'Go therefore and make disciples of all nations, but please leave out the Jews.' For the first time in the sorry history of Christian–Jewish relations, Jews really do seem to have the upper hand.

7
Worship

The Temple

When Moses led the Children of Israel through the wilderness towards the Promised Land, according to the book of Exodus, he made a portable sanctuary. When they settled in camp, this was placed in an open courtyard. The fence surrounding it was made of wooden pillars from which a cloth curtain was suspended. The sanctuary itself was put at the eastern end. It seems to have consisted of two rooms, an ante-chamber and the Holy of Holies. The Ark of the Covenant was kept in the inner sanctum. This was the chest containing the two tablets of stone, on which were written the Ten Commandments. Outside stood the table for the shewbread, the incense altar and the golden-branched candlestick. In the courtyard, there was an outer altar on which sacrifices were offered as well as a brass laver for the use of the priests.

The first Temple in Jerusalem was built by King Solomon in the tenth century BCE. It was on a large scale and it generally followed the pattern of the portable sanctuary. However, it was destroyed by the Babylonians in 586 BCE. By that date, the Ark of the Covenant had already disappeared. Then the Temple was rebuilt by the returning exiles in the late sixth/early fifth centuries and was reconstructed by King Herod (d. 4 BCE) with extraordinary magnificence in the first century. This building was destroyed by the Romans in CE 70.

The Mishnah, which was compiled at the end of the second century CE, contains descriptions of both the structure and the worship of the Temple. By this time the building had consisted of rubble for more than a hundred years, so it is probable that the details are not accurate in every particular. It stood on Mount Moriah in Jerusalem – over the spot where the patriarch Abraham had attempted to sacrifice his son Isaac, the sole heir to the covenant. The large outer court was known as the Court of Gentiles, and this was as far as non-Jews were permitted to go. It seems to have been a busy place and, according to the New Testament, a certain amount of buying and selling took place there. Beyond the Court of the Gentiles was the Court of Women; next in line was the Court of Israelites and then the Court of Priests. Beyond that stood the altar on which the sacrifices were offered. West of the altar was built the Sanctuary with its outer chamber and its Holy of Holies. Thus the hierarchy within the community was established. Only the High Priest could enter the Holy of Holies, and then only twice a year. Since the Ark had been lost, this inner sanctum was totally empty.

According to the book of Deuteronomy, the Temple was the only proper place to offer sacrifice. The entire ritual is described in the talmudic tractate Kodashim. The priests themselves were a hereditary caste, descended from Aaron, the brother of Moses. Today, there are still people in the Jewish community who believe themselves to be Kohenim (members of the priestly caste), but they no longer have many special duties. They are, however, still subject to various ritual laws such as the privilege of being the first to read the Torah and being forbidden to marry a convert or a divorcée. While the Temple stood, they were performing the important function of offering the morning, afternoon and evening sacrifices, saying the regular benedictions and pouring out the drink offerings of wine. Music was provided by a choir of Levites, descendants of Levi, the third son of the patriarch Jacob. Today those who claim to be Levites are called out to read the Torah after the Kohenim, but before the other men.

When the Temple was finally destroyed, only the great Western Wall of the Temple Mount remained. To this day, this is a place of pilgrimage. All Jews who have the least feeling for the traditions of their ancestors want to go to Jerusalem at least once to stand and pray by the Wall. It is largely because of the Wall that the Israelis are reluctant to give up, or even share, the city of Jerusalem. The destruction of the Temple is mourned every year on the ninth day of the month of Av, and it is still anticipated that with the advent of the Messiah the Temple will be raised up again – this time for ever. This hope is expressed in the liturgy: 'Our God and God of our Fathers ... rebuild Thy House ... grant that we may see it in its rebuilding and make us rejoice in its establishment; restore the Kohenim to their service and the Levites to their song and singing, and Israel to their habitations; and there we will go up to appear and worship.'[1]

The synagogue

During the time of the exile in Babylon in the sixth century BCE, the Jews used to meet together to study and pray. They could no longer offer sacrifices because sacrifice was only allowed in the Temple in Jerusalem. Even when the Jews were permitted to return to the Holy Land at the end of the sixth century, many chose to remain in Babylon and others settled in the various urban centres around the Mediterranean Sea. Increasingly, Jewish life revolved around these meeting places, which were known as synagogues. There the people would listen to the scriptures; they would pray together and they would reassert their sense of national and religious identity. So when the Temple was finally destroyed in CE 70 the Jews already had another established institution to nurture their faith.

There are no official laws as to how a synagogue should be built, so generally the architectural details echo the tastes and practices of the time. Medieval synagogues in Europe were built in the Romanesque or Gothic style; there were wooden synagogues in Poland; magnificent revivalist buildings in the nineteenth century and every kind of modernism is represented in the synagogue architecture of the New World. Today synagogues serve as community centres as well as places of worship and study. They have meeting rooms, classrooms, kitchens, libraries, cloakrooms, gift shops and a variety of administrative offices. The regular staff may include a cantor, an educational director, secretaries and janitors as well as one or more rabbis. Volunteers come in and out to supervise children's and young people's activities, to staff the gift shop and to teach various groups. Besides the regular religious services there will be meetings of the Brotherhood and Sisterhood, the various charitable committees, the youth groups and possibly a pre-school. Outside the State of Israel the whole is financed solely by the members. In Israel the Orthodox synagogues are supported by the government, but this is not true of the non-Orthodox who have to rely on their own resources. Families pay substantial sums to join the organization. The staff, including the rabbis, are directly employed by an elected board of lay people. Although most synagogues belong to some umbrella denominational organization, they enjoy almost total independence.

As far as the central sanctuary is concerned, there are a number of elements which parallel Moses' portable shrine and the structure of the Temple in Jerusalem. The focus of the building is a large cupboard in the wall nearest the land of Israel. This is known as the Ark and it is symbolic of the Holy of Holies, the central sanctum of the Temple. Just as the original Ark of the Covenant contained the tablets of the Ten Commandments, so the synagogue Ark contains the scrolls of the Torah. When the doors of the Ark are opened and the scrolls are taken out or put back, the congregation stands as a sign of respect and as an acknowledgement of the central role of Torah in Jewish life. It is considered an honour to be invited to open or close the doors, as it is to be asked to read from the Torah scroll. Scriptural verses which originally referred to the Ark of the Covenant are recited as the Ark doors are opened and closed.

In front of the Ark hangs a lamp. This represents the light that burnt perpetually in the Temple sanctuary. In the centre of the building is a raised platform which is used for the reading of the Torah scroll and from the scriptures, for leading the prayers and perhaps for the sermon. The worshippers sit or stand, facing the Ark and they follow the service in their prayer books. In Orthodox synagogues, men and women sit separately, so that the women do not prove a distraction to the men. Either the women are tucked away in a gallery or they sit behind a heavy curtain. The Conservative and Reform movements, which insist on the absolute equality of men and women, have abolished separate seating in these non-Orthodox synagogues, and families invariably sit together.

For a liturgical service to take place in an Orthodox synagogue there must be at least ten adult men present. Attendance is considered meritorious but, although Jews are enthusiastic builders of synagogues, they are sometimes infrequent attenders. The synagogues are always full on Rosh Hashanah (the New Year) and Yom Kippur (the Day of Atonement), but it is often hard to raise the necessary quorum for the daily services. Nonetheless the synagogue remains the central institution of Jewish life and, according to the Talmud, if a man who is a regular member of the congregation misses a day, then God Himself enquires after him.

Daily prayer

Through the ages, prayer has been the means by which the Jewish people have expressed their deepest emotions. Through their long history of exile, persecution and displacement, they have expressed their joys, sorrows, hopes and despairs both in private prayer and in the words of the established liturgy. Through this personal contact with the Almighty, they have been consoled, sustained and uplifted. In the words of the Psalmist: 'I waited patiently for the Lord; He inclined to me and heard my cry. He drew me up from the desolate pit, out of the miry bog, and set my feet upon a rock, making my steps secure. He put a new song in my mouth, a song of praise to our God' (Psalm 40:1–3).

The three daily services of the synagogue are intended to correspond with the times sacrifices were offered in the Temple in Jerusalem. The morning and afternoon services echo the morning and afternoon sacrifices and the evening prayer service recalls the nightly burning of fats and limbs. It is probable that the essential features of these three synagogue services were established by the sixth century CE, but the traditions were handed down orally from generation to generation. It was only in the eighth century that the first written prayer book was compiled by Rav Amram of Sura in Babylonia. Over the centuries the liturgy grew and developed and different prayers were added by different communities. Today there is a Sephardi (Oriental) and an Ashkenazi (Eastern European) rite; less well known are the prayer-books of the Yemenites and the Italians. In addition, the non-Orthodox movements have produced their own liturgies to reflect their customs and theological priorities. Nonetheless, all these different versions contain several common features.

At the core of the liturgy are two prayers, the Shema and the Amidah. In accordance with the commandment 'You shall teach them diligently to your children, and shall talk of them when you sit in your house, and when you walk by the way, and when you lie down and when you rise' (Deuteronomy 6:7), the community is required to recite the Shema prayer, at the very

least, at the morning and evening service. The prayer consists of
the fundamental declaration of the unity of God: 'Hear O Israel,
the Lord our God, the Lord is One.' It goes on to express the
imperatives of loving God 'with all your heart, and with all your
soul and with all your might' and of the necessity of remembering His words – 'You shall bind them as a sign upon your hand,
and they shall be as frontlets between your eyes. And you shall
write them on the doorposts of your house and on your gates.'[2]
After the first verse, the words 'Blessed be the name of His glorious Kingdom for ever and ever' are added. According to the
second-century law book the Mishnah, reciting the Shema is a
'taking on of the yoke of the Kingdom of Heaven'. It is an asser-
tion of personal faith and an expression of hope in the coming
age when God's Oneness will be acknowledged throughout the
world.

The Amidah consists of eighteen benediction (plus an
additional benediction). The first, remembering the deeds of the
Patriarchs, and the last three, for the restoration of the Temple,
thanking God for His mercies and a request for peace to Israel,
are recited at every service. The other prayers are only said on
weekdays. On the Sabbath, they are replaced by a single prayer
on the blessings of the seventh day. Traditionally the whole of
the Amidah is recited standing, and in the Talmud it is desig-
nated 'ha-Tefillah' – the archetype prayer.

Other important prayers in the daily services are the Kaddish
and the Alenu. The Kaddish expresses the longing for universal
peace in the coming Kingdom of God. This is said at the end of
each major section of the liturgy and is also recited by any
mourners present at the end of the service. The Mourner's
Kaddish can only be recited in a quorum of at least ten men.
Since it is an obligation to 'say Kaddish' for eleven months after
the death of a parent, spouse or sibling, and this custom is widely
observed in the community, it does something to guarantee the
necessary attendance at services. Since the thirteenth century,

the three daily services have concluded with the Alenu prayer. This proclaims God as king over all the world: 'It is our duty to magnify the Lord of the Universe and to acknowledge the greatness of God ... He is our God, there is no other ... Acknowledge it today and take it well into thy heart that God, the Lord, is above in Heaven and down on the earth, He and no other.'[3]

The Sabbath

'Thus the Heavens and the earth were finished ... And on the seventh day God finished His work which He had done, and He rested on the seventh day ... So God blessed the seventh day and hallowed it' (Genesis 2:1–3); 'You shall remember that you were a servant in the land of Egypt and the Lord your God brought you out thence with a mighty hand and an outstretched arm; therefore the Lord your God commanded you to keep the Sabbath day' (Deuteronomy 5:15). The Hebrew scriptures thus give two reasons for keeping the seventh day as a day of rest, firstly because God the Creator Himself rested and secondly in compassion for and in solidarity with the slave labourer.

The idea of a regular day of rest is one of the Jews' great contributions to world civilization. The sages always emphasized that the Sabbath was not merely a day when one refrained from doing things, it was a day of pleasure and delight. It is positively meritorious to make love to one's wife then; it is a time to enjoy friends and family, to study Torah and to worship God. Further, they defined the thirty-nine different types of work which are forbidden and these include writing, baking, kindling a light, sewing, hammering, building, planting or reaping. In today's world, therefore, most do-it-yourself projects are excluded as well as catching up on office work. The housewife also has a rest from the endless round of cooking, shopping, mending and cleaning. The Sabbath begins on Friday evening at sunset. Just before it starts, candles are lit by the mother of the household who recites the benediction 'Blessed art Thou, O Lord our God, King of the Universe, who has sanctified us by Thy commandments and hast commanded us to kindle the Sabbath lights.'⁴ In the synagogue at twilight the Sabbath is welcomed and the famous hymn 'Come my friend to meet the bride; let us welcome the presence of the Sabbath' is recited. On returning home, the father blesses his children, praying to God to make the boys like Ephraim and Menasseh (the two sons of Joseph, favourite son of the patriarch Jacob) and the girls like the matriarchs Sarah, Rebekah, Leah and Rachel. Then he says the Kiddush, the sanctifying prayer, over a cup of wine. This is followed by a ritual washing of the hands and the blessing and sharing of bread.

The Friday night meal is the central family occasion of the week. It is a chance to catch up on family news and to entertain friends and strangers. It is felt that no Jew should be without somewhere to go on a Friday night. After the food has been eaten, special songs are sung and the proceedings conclude with the grace after meals. The rabbis taught that three full meals should be eaten on the Sabbath and it is customary to discuss a religious issue taken from the week's Torah portion. In the synagogue, the liturgy of the morning service includes the prescribed reading from the Torah and another reading from the prophetic literature. The introductory prayers differ from those used on weekdays and the Amidah is shorter. Traditionally seven readers are called up to the central platform for the reading of the Torah and an eighth for the prophetic reading. The liturgy contains several special references to the Sabbath. Again, at the afternoon service, three people are called up for the reading of the Torah and the first section of the next week's Torah portion is also recited. The third meal of the day is eaten just before the end of the Sabbath.

The day concludes with the Havdalah ceremony which generally takes place at home. The term *havdalah* means

'division' and the ritual consists of blessings over wine, spices
and lights: 'Blessed art Thou, O Lord, who makest a distinction
between the holy and the profane, between light and darkness,
between Israel and the peoples, between the seventh day and the
six working days. Blessed art Thou, O Lord, who makest a
distinction between the sacred and the secular.'[5] The spices are
said to refresh the soul, the igniting of the lights indicate that the
Sabbath is over and the ritual is often concluded with the extin-
guishing of the lights by plunging them in the dregs of the wine.
And so the next working week begins.

In an Orthodox household, the regulations are kept strictly.
The family live near the synagogue so they can walk there
without resorting to motorized transport. The electric lights are
on time switches so there is no need to turn them on or off and
all cooking is done earlier and the dishes are left simmering in a
slow oven. For many Jews today all this seems ridiculously
restrictive and old fashioned. Secular and Reform Jews have no
hesitation in using their cars; they may regard the Sabbath as a
time to spend with their family, but they are unbothered by the
niceties of the traditional laws. It is among the Strictly Orthodox
that the true Sabbath spirit prevails. Among a large Orthodox
family sharing the Sabbath meal or out walking together on a
Saturday afternoon, there is a feeling of real tranquillity, prayer-
fulness, family solidarity and joy.

Special Sabbaths

According to the rabbis of the Talmud, the bliss of Sabbath is a
sixtieth part of the bliss reserved for the righteous in the world
to come. The Sabbath is a weekly joy, but some Sabbaths are
regarded as particularly special.

The first group is connected with the new moon. The
Jewish calendar is lunar and each month lasts a little more than

twenty-nine days. Before the fourth century, the authorities had to decide each month whether it was to last twenty-nine or thirty days. The appearance of the new moon marked the start of a new month and, in the days of the Temple, this was celebrated by special sacrifices and a rest from work. Today the new moon is a normal working day, although special prayers are said in the synagogue. The Sabbath before the new moon is known as the Sabbath of Blessing. Worshippers express the hope that it will be God's will to renew the coming month for good service. If the Sabbath falls on the eve of a new moon, then the biblical story of David and Jonathan is read because it took place on a new moon eve (1 Samuel 20:18). If the Sabbath falls on the new moon itself, the Hallel (the Psalms of praise, 113–118) are recited in the synagogue.

There are Sabbaths connected with the major festivals. The Sabbath that falls in the ten days between the New Year and the Day of Atonement is known as the Sabbath of Return or the Sabbath of Repentance. The prophetic reading in the synagogue starts with the words 'Return O Israel to the Lord your God, for you have stumbled because of your iniquity' (Hosea 14:1). During the Sabbath that falls during the intermediate days of Sukkot (the festival of Tabernacles), the Hallel again is recited and the biblical book of Ecclesiastes is read after the morning service. On the Sabbath of Genesis, which follows the festival of Rejoicing in the Law (Simhat Torah) at the end of Sukkot, the annual cycle of Torah reading begins. It is a particular honour to be called up to read on this Sabbath and whoever is chosen often provides a festival meal for all to share after the service.

The Sabbath of Hanukkah (the festival of Lights) is the Sabbath that falls during the eight days of the festival and again the Hallel is said in the synagogue. The Sabbath of Song is celebrated when the Torah portion includes the Song of Moses which the Children of Israel sang after they had crossed the Red Sea (Exodus 15:1–18). In some congregations special religious poems are also recited. The Sabbath of the Shekel Tax comes round in the spring. It has its origin in the annual warning that the tax to support the Temple was due. Today the congregation is frequently urged to make a contribution to a religious institution in Israel. Also in the spring is the Sabbath of Remembrance, which is the Sabbath before Purim, the feast of Esther. During the service the people are urged to 'remember what Amalek [the ancestor of Haman, the villain of the book of Esther] did to you'. The Sabbath of the Red Heiffer recalls the ritual of purification used in the Temple and the following Sabbath is known as the Sabbath of the Month and is the Sabbath immediately before the start of the month in which the great festival of Passover takes place.

The Sabbath that precedes Passover is known as the Great Sabbath. Usually the rabbi gives a lecture on the coming festival and the preparations for it that have to be made. On the Sabbath that takes place during the intermediate days of the Passover festival, the Hallel is said and the biblical Song of Songs is recited after the morning service. The Sabbath that precedes the ninth day of Av, the day of mourning for the destruction of the Temple, is known as the Sabbath of Prophecy. Congregants attend synagogue in plainer clothes than usual and the Ark in the synagogue is draped with a black curtain. The following Sabbath is called the Sabbath of Comfort and the people are consoled with the prophetic reading 'Comfort, comfort my people, says your God' (Isaiah 40:1).

Many of these Sabbaths are no longer observed by non-Orthodox Jews. For the Strictly Orthodox, however, life is punctuated by the regular day of rest and the special Sabbaths of the liturgical year. The rhythm provides a predictable and reassuring background to the pleasures and pains, skirmishes and dramas of everyday living.

8
Festivals

The Jewish year

Because the Jewish year is lunar and the secular calendar is solar, the Jewish festivals do not occur on the same date every secular year. The twelve lunar months only contain 354 days. The shortfall is made up by adding a thirteenth month periodically. So, although the festivals occur on different dates, they do come round at roughly the same time of year – Passover is a spring festival, Tabernacles occurs in the autumn and the feast of Esther in late winter/early spring.

According to the book of Deuteronomy, the Jewish people are to celebrate three pilgrim festivals each year: 'Three times a year all your males shall appear before the Lord your God at the place which He will choose; at the festival of unleavened bread [Passover], at the feast of Weeks and at the feast of booths [Tabernacles]. They shall not appear before the Lord empty-handed' (Deuteronomy 16:16). In the days of the Temple, large numbers of pilgrims went to Jerusalem to offer sacrifice. All three festivals are connected with the agricultural year as well as with important events in the history of the Jews. Passover celebrates the start of the barley harvest and the liberation from slavery in Egypt; Weeks involves the offering of the first fruits as well as commemorating the giving of the Torah to Moses on Mount Sinai; and Tabernacles is a harvest festival and a remembrance of the sojourn in the wilderness.

An overview of the calendar:

Season	Month	Date	Festival
Spring	Nisan	15–22	Passover (Pesah)
	Iyyar	5	Israel Independence Day
		18	Lag ba-Omer
	Shivan	6–7	Weeks (Shavuot)
Summer	Tammuz	17	Fast of Tammuz
	Av	9	Fast of Av
	Elul		
Autumn	Tishri	1–2	New Year (Rosh Hashanah)
		1–10	Ten Days of Penitence
		3	Fast of Gedaliah
		10	Day of Atonement (Yom Kippur)
		15–21	Tabernacles (Sukkot)
	Marheshvan		
	Kislev	25–2/3	Lights (Hanukkah)
Winter	Tevet	10	Fast of 10 Tevet
	Shevat	15	New Year for Trees
	Adar	14	Esther (Purim)

The scriptures also command the Jews: 'In the seventh month, on the first day of the month, you shall observe a day of solemn rest, a memorial proclaimed with blast of trumpets, a holy convocation' (Leviticus 23:24). This is kept as the New Year. Ten days later comes the most sacred day of the whole year:

> On the tenth day of the seventh month is the Day of Atonement; it shall be for you a time of holy convocation, and you shall afflict yourself and present an offering by fire to the Lord and you shall do no work on this same day; for it is a day of atonement for you before the Lord your God. (Leviticus 23:27–8)

These ten days are known as the Ten Days of Penitence.

Other festivals and fasts came into the Jewish calendar after the biblical period. Israel Independence Day is a celebration of the State of Israel's declaration of independence in 1948; Lag ba-Omer commemorates the ending of a plague in the second century CE; the festival of Lights (Hanukkah) celebrates the re-dedication of the Temple by Judah Maccabee after the Seleucid dynasty was defeated in 165 BCE; the New Year for Trees is a joyous minor agricultural festival; and the feast of Esther (Purim) is a time of rejoicing at the defeat of Haman's plot to destroy the Jewish people. The fasts include 17 Tammuz, which mourns the day when the walls of Jerusalem were breached by the Romans; on 9 Av the community remembers the destruction of the Temple first by the Babylonian King Nebuchadnezzar in the sixth century BCE and then by the Romans in the first century CE; the fast of Gedaliah commemorates the assassination of Gedaliah, the governor of the Jews appointed by Nebuchadnezzar and 10 Tevet recalls the siege of Jerusalem by the Babylonian king.

On major festivals work is forbidden except for that connected with the preparation of food, which is permitted. On the minor festivals, such as Purim and Hanukkah, there are no such prohibitions. Traditionally, all the festivals, except for the Day of Atonement, are kept for two days. This originates in the annual practice of determining the start of each new month by the sighting of the new moon. It took time for the news to reach the communities of the dispersion so the festivals were celebrated on both possible days. Many Reform Congregations have abolished this custom and follow the ancient practice of only observing them for the one day.

Passover

The festival of Passover has several different dimensions. According to the book of Exodus, God sent ten plagues to the land of Egypt to compel the Egyptian king to let his Israelite slaves leave. The final plague was the death of the first-born. All the eldest children and all the first-born animals mysteriously died. Only the Israelites were spared. They had been instructed that each household should slaughter a lamb and daub its blood on the doorposts of their houses. When the Angel of Death saw the blood, he 'passed over' that house. In the days of the Temple, lambs were slaughtered at the beginning of the festival and were roasted and eaten with bitter herbs. The Samaritans carry on this practice to the present day.

The festival is also known as the festival of Unleavened Bread. Once the king gave permission for the Israelites to go, they were in such a hurry that they did not even wait for their bread to rise. God commanded that no leaven was to be eaten at future Passover celebrations and that none should be kept in the house for the duration of the festival. Consequently, it is the custom just before the festival to conduct a thorough spring-clean. All leavened goods are removed, special Passover cutlery and crockery are brought out and a final ritual 'search for leaven' is carried out. The last symbolic crumbs are swept into a spoon with a feather. Although their Christian neighbours ascribed it to sorcery, the notorious good health of the Jewish community in the Middle Ages may partly have been due to this annual rite of cleanliness.

Passover is also described as the festival of Spring – referring back to its traditional agricultural connections and as the Season of our Freedom. Primarily the festival is a celebration of liberation; as the liturgy puts it: 'Then we were slaves, now we are free men ...'[1] Traditionally it is kept for seven days in Israel and eight in the Dispersion and its main focus is the Passover Seder (meal) which takes place on the first (and also the second) night. Even the most secular Jews often attend a Passover Seder and most have vivid childhood memories of the occasion. It is an opportunity for the extended family to get together – grandparents, aunts and uncles, miscellaneous cousins, parents and children. The nearest parallel in Christian circles is Christmas dinner. It is a huge amount of work for the host and inevitably all the tensions, as well as all the joys, of family life emerge.

The meal fulfils the commandment in the book of Exodus 'And you shall tell your son on that day; it is because of what the Lord did for me when I went out of Egypt' (13:18). On the table is placed an array of symbolic food. There are three pieces of *matzot* (unleavened bread). The top and bottom represent the double portion of manna which was provided for the Israelites on their wanderings in the wilderness. The middle piece is divided in two; one part is described as the 'bread of affliction' reminding the participants of the miseries of slavery while the other is set aside and hidden. This is a device to amuse the children. It is eaten after the meal, recalling Temple times when the meal concluded with the eating of the Passover lamb.

Also laid out are bitter herbs (generally horseradish) representing the bitterness of slavery, the green herb associated with the spring, salt water representing the tears of the Israelite slaves, *haroset* (a mixture of apples, nuts, cinnamon and wine) reminiscent of the mortar the Jews were compelled to mix in Egypt, a roasted bone symbolizing the Passover sacrifice and an egg commemorating the festival sacrifice in the Temple. Also on the table is the cup of Elijah. According to tradition, the Messiah will reveal himself at Passover time and the prophet Malachi promises that he will be heralded by the prophet Elijah. During the course of the evening, the front door is opened in the hope that this year, at long last, Elijah will be waiting. Each participant drinks four cups of wine. These are linked with the four expressions of redemption in the book of Exodus, 'I will bring you out ... I will deliver you ... and I will redeem you ... and I will take you for My people' (6:6–7).

During the course of the evening, blessings are said, the symbolic food is eaten and the Passover story is told. Then the full meal is eaten. This is followed by grace after the meal, the reciting of the Hallel (Psalms 113–18), a concluding liturgy and the singing of various songs and hymns. The service ends with the long-cherished hope, 'Next Year in Jerusalem'. The evening lasts for a long time and it is unquestionably one of the most poignant and memorable occasions of the Jewish year.

Weeks

The barley harvest offering was brought on the second day of Passover. According to the book of Leviticus, 'You shall count from the morrow after the Sabbath, from the day that you brought the sheaf of the wave offering; seven full weeks shall they be, counting fifty days to the morrow after the seventh Sabbath ... And you shall make proclamation on the same day, you shall hold a holy convocation' (23:15, 21). The barley harvest sheaf was known as the Omer and, after the destruction of the Temple in CE 70, it became the custom for each individual to count the days of the Omer, marking the passing of the weeks from the Festival of the Passover to that of Weeks.

In the days of the Temple, the fifty days of the Omer were a joyful period. Later it became a time of mourning. No one knows exactly why the change took place, but among the Orthodox, except on Lag ba-Omer (the thirty-third day), no marriages take place and it is forbidden to have a haircut. However, the seven weeks are punctuated by two other festivals. Since 1948, Israel Independence Day is celebrated on the fifth day of the month of Iyyar; thirteen days later, the traditional feast of Lag ba-Omer takes place. Lag ba-Omer goes back to the time of the great Babylonian talmudic academies of Sura and Pumbedita which flourished from the seventh to the eleventh centuries. It commemorates the ending of a plague among the disciples of the second-century scholar Rabbi Akiva. Traditionally teachers took their students out for a day in the country where they held bow-and-arrow contests. Also, Simeon ben Yohai (second century CE), the putative author of the *Zohar*, an important mystical work, is said to have died on Lag ba-Omer. Since the seventeenth century, pilgrimages have been made to his grave and today bonfires are lit throughout the land of Israel in his honour. Among the Strictly Orthodox, it is the time for small boys to have their first haircuts and it is the one day during the counting of the Omer when marriages may be celebrated.

After the forty-nine days, the seven weeks, have been counted, the festival of Weeks (Shavuot in Hebrew) is celebrated. This feast is also known as Pentecost from the Greek word for 'fifty'. Originally it was an agricultural festival and, with Passover and Tabernacles, was an occasion for pilgrimage to the Jerusalem Temple. In the book of Leviticus, the people are commanded to 'present a cereal offering of new grain to the Lord. You shall bring from your dwellings two loaves of bread to be waved and made of two lengths of an ephah; they shall be of fine flour and they shall be baked with leaven, a first-fruit to the Lord' (23:17). Later, because the Children of Israel were said to have arrived at Mount Sinai with Moses in the third month (that is the month of Shivan), it became a commemoration of the giving of the Torah to the Jewish people.

In the liturgy, the festival of Weeks is described as 'the season of the giving of our Torah'.[2] In some communities, it is usual to stay awake during the night of the feast; in the synagogue prayers from the Talmud and other rabbinical materials are read. In the Dispersion, where the festival is celebrated for two days, on the second night passages are taken from the book of Psalms. During the services, the liturgical readings include the Ten Commandments, and the book of Ruth is also heard. This is because Ruth, as a convert, of her own free will took on the yoke of the Torah. For the same reason, the festival marks the graduation of young people from formal synagogue education and, among the non-Orthodox, the ceremony of confirmation has been introduced for sixteen-year-olds as an incentive for the boys and girls to stay in religion school beyond their bar or bat mitzvah celebration three years earlier.

It is the custom to eat dairy products during the festival of Weeks. Various suggestions have been made as to the reason for this – perhaps the most convincing is that the Torah is like milk; it nourishes everyone from the very young to the very old. In addition, the synagogue is decorated with fruit and flowers, symbolizing the beauty and the fragrance of the law. It has to be said that some later authorities have objected to this custom as being too reminiscent of the Christian harvest festival. In general, this morose view is ignored and the festival is a time of joy and merriment.

Tabernacles

The third pilgrim festival, Tabernacles (Sukkot in Hebrew), is also prescribed in the scriptures:

> On the fifteenth day of the seventh month and for seven days is the feast of booths [Tabernacles] to the Lord. On the first day shall be a holy convocation; you shall do no laborious work. Seven days you shall present offerings by fire to the Lord; on the eighth day you shall hold a holy convocation and present an offering by fire to the Lord; it is a solemn assembly; you shall do no laborious work. (Leviticus 23:33–6)

Later, it is described how

> you shall take on the first day the fruit of goodly trees, branches

of palm trees and boughs of leafy trees and willows of the
brook; and you shall rejoice before the Lord your God for
seven days ... You shall dwell in booths for seven days ... that
your generation may know that I made the people of Israel
dwell in booths when I brought them up out of the land of
Egypt. (Leviticus 23:40, 42, 43)

Thus the feast of Tabernacles was ordained to remind the Jews
of their sojourn in the wilderness before they reached the
Promised Land, a time when they were particularly close to
God. Even today they are expected to build their own tabernacle (*sukkah*) and the sages of the Talmud explained in detail how
it is to be done. It has to be at least four square cubits in size (a
cubit is about one-and-a-half feet); it must have at least three
walls and it must have a covering of things that were once
growing. This does not mean that it should have a complete
roof; when the pious Jew stands in his tabernacle, he should be
able to see the stars through the branches or straw of the covering. Main meals should be eaten in the structure for the duration
of the festival, but, in colder climates, there is no obligation to
sleep in it or even to stay in it if it rains.

In addition, it is necessary to obey the commandment of
taking the fruit and the branches; this is done by holding a citron
in one hand and branches of palm, willow and myrtle (collectively known as the *lulav*) in the other. During the liturgical
services in the synagogue, the *lulav* is waved in six directions,
north, south, east, west, up and down. Probably this symbolizes
God's control of all the points of the compass and all space.
Various explanations have been given as to the composition of
the *lulav* – perhaps the most attractive is that it symbolizes the
very different types of Jews that make up the community, that
all are necessary and that all should work in harmony while
keeping their individuality. In any event, the *lulav* is waved
while the Hallel (Psalms 113–18) is recited and it is taken in a

circuit around the synagogue while a prayer is said for a good harvest.

On the seventh day of the festival, which is known as the Great Hoshanah ('God Saves'), seven circuits are made. This is often perceived as the culmination of the whole season of repentance (the New Year, the Ten Days of Penitence and the Day of Atonement) which have gone before. Since it is celebrated during the course of the Tabernacles festival, it is a mixture of both joy and solemnity. The next day, the day of the holy convocation, is Shemini Atzeret (the eighth day of the solemn assembly) and Simhat Torah (the Rejoicing in the Law). Traditionally in Israel, and among Reform Jews, both festivals are commemorated on the same day, but generally in the Dispersion, because the whole festival of Tabernacles lasts an extra day, Shemini Atzeret is celebrated on the eighth day and Simhat Torah on the ninth. No work is permitted and on Shemini Atzeret a prayer for rain is recited.

The Day of Rejoicing in the Law is a time of great joy. The annual reading of the Torah is completed and the whole cycle begins again with the first portion from the book of Genesis. It is considered to be a great honour to be called up for the final reading from the book of Deuteronomy and the man chosen is given the title of 'Bridegroom of the Torah'. His successor, who is called up for the Genesis reading, is known as the 'Bridegroom of Genesis'. During the course of the service, the scrolls of the Torah are taken from the Ark and are carried in procession around the synagogue amidst laughter and exultation. In Hasidic communities particularly, the enthusiasm is overwhelming and the procession spills out onto the street amid singing and dancing. The children of the congregation are also called up and are given sweets and fruit and they too join the procession, carrying flags. In many communities it is the custom for the two 'bridegrooms' to give a party for the whole community and often this is a sumptuous feast. Nothing is considered too good to express joy in God's gift to His Chosen People, His Torah.

Lights and Esther

The festival of Lights, known in Hebrew as Hanukkah, is celebrated for eight days beginning on 25 Kislev. It commemorates an episode in Jewish history in which the intensely devout Maccabee family overcame the Greek ruling Seleucid dynasty in the second century BCE. The Seleucids had desecrated the Temple in Jerusalem and had forbidden the practice of the Jewish religion. After a three-year struggle, in 165 BCE, Judah Maccabee captured the city and rebuilt the altar in the Temple. According to talmudic legend, one day's worth of sacred oil miraculously kept the golden candelabrum burning for eight days. The festival celebrates this miracle.

Commemoration centres on the lighting of the Hanukkah lights. On the first evening one candle or lamp is ignited, on the second night two, and so on for eight days. The candles are lit after sunset (except on the Sabbath when they must be lit before the Sabbath candles) by means of an additional light known as the serving light (*shammash*). The kindling should go from right to left. In the synagogue the Hallel (Psalms 113–18) is recited and special prayers are said.

However, it is primarily a home festival and in recent years has assumed considerable importance. This is because it occurs round about Christmas time and it is used to protect children from being enticed by the whole commercial onslaught of the 'festive season'. Jewish young people are told that while Christians celebrate Christmas, Jews have Hanukkah. They receive a present(s) for every night of the festival. Parties are held which include games and singing. The best-known game involves a spinning top which is inscribed with four Hebrew letters forming an acrostic for the Hebrew phrase meaning 'a great miracle occurred here'. It is customary to eat potato pancakes and sugar doughnuts and, even at home, the hymn '*Maoz Tsur*' (Rock of Ages) or Psalm 30 is sung. Even fairly secular households have Hanukkah candlesticks and some attempt is made to provide the children with an alternative jollification to the all-pervasive Christmas festivities. Inevitably in such families, Christian (or pagan) customs do creep in. It is not unusual to find something that looks to the uneducated eye exactly like a Christmas tree, but which is determinedly referred to as a Hanukkah bush!

The feast of Esther (Purim in Hebrew), is celebrated on 14 Adar. This commemorates the deliverance of the Persian Jews at the intercession of the Jewish queen, Esther, from the murderous plans of Haman, the chief minister of King Ahasuerus, the story of which is to be found in the biblical book of Esther. The term Purim comes from the Hebrew word for 'lot' and refers to Haman's casting of lots to determine a date for the destruction of the Jewish people. In remembrance of this the fast of Esther is observed on 13 Adar because, in the story, Queen Esther proclaimed a fast before she interceded with the king for the lives of her co-religionists. The celebrations take place the next day and, according to the biblical account, the festival was inaugurated by Esther's cousin Mordecai in thanksgiving for their deliverance.

Traditionally the festival is celebrated in the synagogue. In both the evening and the morning service, the book of Esther, written on a single scroll, is chanted to a traditional melody. In many congregations, the occasion resembles a carnival. The children dress up as Esther or Mordecai, the heroine and hero of the tale. Whenever Haman's name is mentioned, an attempt is made to drown it by foot-stamping or by whirling noisemakers. Little plays are put on and students in talmudic academies have licence to imitate the foibles of their teachers. During the course of the service a special prayer of thanksgiving is said and, after the morning service, a special festive meal takes place. This often includes a confection known as Hamantashen (Haman's hats). These are triangular pastries with poppyseed and dried fruit. It is also usual for parents to give children little gifts of money, and presents are sent to close friends and to the poor. It is also said that so much wine should be drunk that the imbiber should no longer be able to distinguish between the names of Haman and Mordecai – and in a few circles this provision is still taken literally.

The festival of Esther, like the festival of Lights, is only a minor feast, but in modern times it has also assumed considerable importance. Possibly this is because carnival customs have been adopted. In the state of Israel, parades take place with revellers dressed in Purim costumes. In its early days, the Reform movement frowned on the festival as being too nationalistic and vindictive in orientation (at the end of the story Haman and his sons are hanged from the highest gallows). However, popular appeal was too great and today Reform temples hold readings of the scroll of Esther with all the accompanying noise in a manner indistinguishable from the Orthodox. In addition, other special Purims are celebrated by particular Jewish communities to celebrate times in their own history when they were delivered from danger. The message of all these occasions is clear. Even at times of greatest danger, God is at work and, in His own mysterious way, He is striving to preserve His own people.

9
Fasts

Sin and forgiveness

In the Hebrew scriptures, sin is understood as a transgression against the decrees of God. It involves falling short of the perfection demanded by the Almighty in His Torah and it indicates that the relationship between God and humanity has broken down. It is characterized by waywardness, failure and undesirable behaviour. A sinner is one who has not fulfilled either his ritual or his moral obligations and there is an acknowledgement in the text that human beings are inclined to evil – 'the wickedness of man was great in the earth and that every imagination of the thoughts of his heart was only evil continually' (Genesis 6:5). Constant vigilance is required from each human being to overcome this evil inclination. Only through willing submission to the provisions of the Torah can the Jewish people be liberated from their natural sinful impulses. However, once sin has been committed, various measures are available to mitigate its consequences.

In the days when the Temple was still standing in Jerusalem, sacrifices were offered daily. According to the 'Ethics of the Fathers', a tractate of the Mishnah, 'the world stands on three things, on Torah, on the Temple service and on loving kindness'. These Temple sacrifices were ordained by God and were perceived as means by which the guilt of sin could be wiped away. According to the twelfth-century philosopher Abraham ibn Ezra, through sacrifice the sinner symbolically experienced the death he deserved for his evil deeds. However, several of the biblical prophets railed against the practice: 'I hate, I despise your feasts and I take no delight in your solemn assemblies. Even though you offer me your burnt offerings and cereal offerings, I will not accept them, and the peace offerings of your fatted beasts I will not look upon' (Amos 5:21–2). This was because the people seem to have felt that their sacrifices blotted out their bad deeds and that they therefore could continue with their iniquities with impunity. Amos knew that more was required. His words thunder down the ages: 'Let justice roll down like waters and righteousness like an everflowing stream' (5:24).

Even while sacrifices were being offered, the prophets stressed the importance of true repentance. In order to achieve forgiveness, the sinner must turn from his evil ways and return to God. It requires far more than sacrifice. What is necessary is remorse, restitution and a determination not to repeat the offence. Once the Temple had been destroyed in CE 70, repentance and atonement were the only mechanism by which the relationship with God could be restored. The rabbis of the talmudic period made many statements on the subject, and these were summarized by the twelfth-century philosopher and codifier Maimonides. He asserted that as there is no longer a Temple in Jerusalem, repentance alone atones for sin. The wrongdoer must confess his sins to God and must promise never again to commit them. The test of true repentance is if the sinner has the opportunity of repeating his sin, but refrains from doing so. Then, in addition to confession, when the sin was against another human being, the sinner must make full restitution and must directly ask for forgiveness. Anything that was stolen must be restored. Attempts must be made to soothe hurt feelings and restore broken relationships.

The thirteenth-century devotional writer Jonah ben Abraham Gerondi suggested among the factors of true repentance the following: remorse, shame, submission to God, confession, prayer, compensating the victim, almsgiving, asceticism, reflection on suitable punishments and affliction of the body through fasting and weeping. Fasting, in particular, is regarded as making atonement for sin, and it may involve abstention not only from food, but also from drink, from sexual relations and from wearing leather. In fact, the sages did not stress the virtues of asceticism. Maimonides himself did not mention that any form of physical mortification was necessary if pardon was to be achieved, and later religious authorities, such as Ezekiel Landau of Prague (1713–93), insisted that fasting is only secondary and that basically repentance involves relinquishment of the sin, confession and sincere remorse.

However, the community takes the duty of fasting seriously. Days are set aside in the calendar as community fasts and even the most secular Jew is aware when the great season of repentance arrives in the autumn. It starts with the New Year and concludes ten days later with the Day of Atonement. It is a solemn and serious time, but Jews are promised that it will not be for ever. One day, in the glorious future, 'Thus says the Lord: the fast(s) ... shall be to the house of Judah seasons of joy and gladness and cheerful feasts' (Zechariah 8:19).

The New Year

The New Year (Rosh Hashanah) is observed for two days on the first and second of the month of Tishri. It marks the start of the Ten Days of Penitence which end on the Day of Atonement (Yom Kippur). In the Bible the festival is described as a Day of Solemn Rest, a Day of Memorial to be proclaimed with the blast of a horn and as a Day of Blowing the Horn. In the post-biblical era, it was known as the Day of Remembrance and the Day of Judgement. According to the book of Numbers, 'On the first day of the seventh month, you shall have a holy convocation; you shall do no laborious work. It is a day for you to blow the trumpets' (29:1).

The Mishnah teaches that all human beings pass before God on the New Year – consequently self-examination is an essential element of the day. It is said that every individual stands before the throne of God and is subject to judgement. A very small proportion are judged to be fully righteous and another tiny group is rejected as irredeemably wicked. The vast majority, however, are of the middling sort. They have the Ten Days of Penitence to repent of their folly and evil ways because final judgement is not sealed until the Day of Atonement. For ten days their fate hangs in the balance and, in view of the seriousness of the situation, these ten days are also known as the Days of Awe.

In the synagogue, the Ark, the reading desk and the Torah scrolls are all decked in white. Among Eastern European Jews, it is customary for the rabbi and cantor who lead the services also to wear white robes. Many Jews spend all day in the synagogue, and the liturgy includes references to God's sovereignty, providence and revelation. The emphasis is on the vocation of the Jewish people. The Torah readings include the story of the birth of Isaac, the son of Abraham, and his attempted sacrifice. The prophetic passages depict the birth of the prophet Samuel, who was dedicated from the womb to God's service and with Jeremiah's prophecy of the final restoration of Israel. Most evocative, however, is the blowing of the shofar. A shofar is a trumpet made out of a ram's horn. It produces a strange, unearthly sound. According to the book of Joshua, its notes, coupled with the shouts of the people, caused the walls of the city of Jericho to fall down flat. During the service it is blown repeatedly at three points: after the reading of the law; during and after the additional service; and before the concluding prayer. The precise form of blowing is laid down and is a combination of long notes, tremulous notes and short blasts. According to the twelfth-century philosopher Moses Maimonides, it is blown to call sinners to repentance. As he explains in his code of law, the shofar is commanding: 'Awake you sinners and ponder your deeds; remember your Creator, forsake your evil ways and return to God.'[1] The service concludes with the promise that repentance, prayer and charity can avert the evil decree.

It is a custom among the Strictly Orthodox to go to the seaside or a river bank on the afternoon of the first day and symbolically cast sin away into the water (the ceremony of Tashlikh). Prayers are said for divine forgiveness and verses from the book of Micah are recited: 'Who is God like Thee pardoning iniquity and passing over transgression for the remnant of His inheritance ... He will again have compassion upon us ... Thou wilt cast all our sins into the depths of the sea' (5:18–19). At home, after the blessing over the wine and the sanctification prayer, bread and apples are dipped in honey and a prayer is recited asking that the year ahead may be good and sweet. On the second night of New Year, it is a custom to eat of the new season's fruit while thanking God for preservation to this season. The special bread baked is either round, representing the hope of a good round year, or it has a plaited crust shaped like a ladder; this symbolizes the effort of directing the individual's life to God.

The New Year is a solemn festival, but it is not strictly a fast day. Nonetheless, it heralds a serious time. During the following ten days a number of additions are made to the liturgy and it is usual to visit the graves of close relatives. This is a preparation for the most holy day of the Jewish year, the Day of Atonement.

The Day of Atonement

Like the New Year, the Day of Atonement (Yom Kippur) is prescribed in scripture. According to the book of Numbers: 'On the tenth day of this seventh month, you shall have a holy convocation, and afflict yourselves; you shall do no work, but you shall offer a burnt offering to the Lord, a pleasing odour'

(29:7–8). According to the book of Leviticus, the High Priest wore a plain linen garment and offered a bull as a sin offering. He also cast lots between two goats; one was sacrificed there and then and the other, the scapegoat, was sent away into the wilderness, carrying the sins of the people with it. This was the one day of the year that the Holy of Holies in the Temple was entered. The High Priest would go in to pray for forgiveness for the Jewish nation.

It is said that the Day of Atonement is the anniversary of Moses' return from the summit of Mount Sinai with the second tablets of stone and the news that God had forgiven His people for the sin of the golden calf. It is a solemn day of self-denial. Every male over the age of thirteen and every female over twelve, unless there is a medical reason against it, is obliged to fast from sunset until nightfall the next day. The usual laws of fasting apply, and the rabbis taught that through this affliction atonement could be made for sins against God. Transgressions against others, however, can only receive pardon if forgiveness has been sought from the person injured. Therefore, just before the Day of Atonement, it is usual for people to seek reconciliation with anyone whom they might have offended. In some congregations, it is also customary to slaughter a fowl, sell it and give away the money to charity. Its death symbolizes the transfer of guilt from the sinner to the dead bird. The Reform movement and many of the modern Orthodox have completely abandoned this practice and content themselves with giving money to charity.

During the course of the Day itself, five services take place, all with their characteristic liturgies. The evening of the fast is known as Kol Nidre (All the vows) after the prayer which begins the great service. Among the Orthodox, it was a common practice to spend the night in the synagogue, reciting the entire book of Psalms. The liturgy centres around the confession of sin, always using the first person plural pronoun emphasizing collective responsibility: 'Our Father, Our King, we have sinned against You ...' Besides the penitential prayers and hymns, the morning service includes a Torah reading describing how the Day was celebrated in the Temple, a reading from the book of Numbers concerning festival sacrifice and a prophetic reading from the book of Isaiah describing the true meaning of fasting: 'Is it not to share your bread with the hungry, and bring the homeless poor into your house ... Then shall your light break forth like the dawn and your healing shall spring up speedily' (58:7–8).

In the additional service, the leader chants the order of worship in the Temple and describes how the High Priest, on this one day of the year, would utter the ineffable name of God. In many Orthodox congregations, the worshippers kneel and prostrate themselves at this point. This is the only time that Jews kneel for prayer. Later a martyrology is recited; this describes the plight of the ten martyrs who defied the Emperor Hadrian's ban on studying Torah. In recent years, readings from Holocaust sources have been introduced at this point. During the afternoon service the Leviticus list of forbidden marriages is recited and the second reading is from the book of Jonah, emphasizing the presence of God and the value of true repentance. The long day ends with a final concluding service. Worshippers ask God to inscribe each individual for a good life and to seal them for a favourable fate. It ends with the recital of the first words of the Shema – 'Hear O Israel, the Lord our God, the Lord is One.' This is followed by the threefold recitation of 'Blessed be the name of His glorious kingdom for ever' and the sevenfold declaration: 'The Lord He is God, the Lord He is God.' After saying the usual weekday evening service, a single note from the ram's horn is sounded. The Day of Atonement has come to an end.

Synagogues are full on the New Year and the Day of Atonement. Jews who never go at any other time remain fascinated by the ancient ritual. Ultimately, for all its solemnity, the

Day of Atonement is a time of joy because the Jewish people are reconciled with God. After nightfall a large meal is eaten to break the fast and there is joy and merriment. According to a well-known midrash (biblical comment) at the end of the Day of Atonement, a heavenly voice can be heard quoting from the book of Ecclesiastes, 'Go thy way, eat thy bread with enjoyment and drink your wine with a merry heart; for God has already approved what you do' (9:7).

Other fasts

The other fasts in the Jewish year commemorate tragic events in the nation's history. Most significant is that of the ninth day of Av (Tishah b'Av). This was the day when Nebuchadnezzar, king of Babylon, destroyed the Temple in Jerusalem in 586 BCE, and it is also the anniversary of the devastation of the Second Temple by Titus, who was later to become emperor of Rome. In addition, according to the Mishnah, it was on this day that God decreed that the older Israelites would not live to enter the Promised Land as a punishment for their murmurings against Him. It is also remembered as the day on which Jerusalem was ploughed up on the orders of the Emperor Hadrian in CE 135 after the Bar Kokhba Revolt. Thus it is a time of great sadness. As a sign of mourning, a modified fast period is kept between the first day of Av and the day of the fast itself. Except for on the Sabbath, no meat or wine should be consumed. The fast itself begins at sunset on the eighth day of Av and, like the Day of Atonement, it lasts for the full twenty-five hours. In the synagogue, the members of the congregation remove their shoes and sit on low chairs, as is the custom for mourners. The Ark is stripped of its curtain and covering and the book of Lamentations is chanted, together with other tragic dirges.

The leaders of the Reform movement abolished the fast on the grounds that they no longer expect or desire the rebuilding of the Temple. Once the State of Israel was re-established, even some of the Orthodox felt that there was no longer any need to mourn on the ninth of Av. Nonetheless, the fast has retained its popularity. According to legend, the Messiah will be born on the fast day – and this seems fitting in view of his mission to restore the Temple and the sacrificial system. The month after Av is Elul. This is the final month of the year and, as a preparation for the New Year, the Days of Penitence and the Day of Atonement, it is customary to be particularly conscientious about religious observance. Between the ninth of Av and the New Year, the prophetic readings in the synagogue are passages of consolation taken from the book of Isaiah. For all the sorrows of the ninth of Av, Jews cling to the hope that God will remain faithful to His people.

The seventeenth of Tammuz commemorates the breaching of the walls of Jerusalem, first by the Babylonians in 586 BCE and later by the Romans in CE 70. Other disasters are also connected with the date. According to the Mishnah, it was the day on which Moses broke the Tablets of the Law when he saw the Israelites worshipping the golden calf; it is the anniversary of the last burnt offering in the Temple during the Roman siege and, earlier, a Syrian general named Apostomus burnt the Torah and set up an idol in the sanctuary. The fast begins at sunrise of the day itself (rather than on the previous evening) and, in the synagogue, readings are taken from the book of Exodus concerning the golden calf and the obstinacy of the people.

Another minor fast is that of the tenth of Tevet. This commemorates the start of the siege of Jerusalem by King Nebuchadnezzar. Again it begins at dawn and ends at nightfall and the liturgy includes penitential prayers. The readings in the synagogue include Moses' prayer for the forgiveness of the nation. In the state of Israel, 10 Tevet is observed as a day of remembrance for the six million Jews who died in the Nazi Holocaust.

The fast of Gedaliah, which takes place on the third of Tishri, commemorates the murder of Gedaliah, the Jewish governor of Judah appointed by King Nebuchadnezzar. Even though the majority of the population had already been taken into exile, enough remained possibly to rebuild the Temple. However, after Gedaliah's assassination, the remainder fled to Egypt. Thus during the fast, the exile is remembered and mourned. Again, fasting lasts from dawn to dusk and penitential hymns are recited in the synagogue.

The rabbis suggested other fasts in addition to these official fast days. They recommended fasting on the first Monday and Thursday and on the following Monday after the festivals of Passover and Tabernacles, on the last day of each month and on the seventh of Adar, which is the traditional date of the death of Moses. It is also customary to fast on the anniversary of the death of a parent or teacher, on one's wedding day and if a Torah scroll is dropped.

Fasting customs

In the Hebrew scriptures, we read of the nation fasting for seven days after the death of King Saul (1 Samuel 31:13) and King David praying and fasting in order to persuade God to spare the life of his child (1 Samuel 12:16). Fasting was clearly a common response to a calamity or seen as a means of obtaining divine forgiveness. The only official early fast day mentioned in the Bible was the Day of Atonement. The other fast days came into the calendar in response to and in commemoration of natural disasters. However, after the exile in Babylon, formal fasts were introduced. The prophet Zechariah, working in the sixth century BCE, writes of 'the fast of the fourth month and the fast of the fifth and the fast of the seventh and the fast of the tenth' (8:19). It seems that the practice of fasting, which had in the early days been a spontaneous reaction to disaster, became institutionalized as a series of regular annual events.

The legal sources lay down a series of prescriptions which must be followed when fasting. In the early days fasting seems to have been accompanied by sacrifice, confession and prayer. King David is described as beseeching God for his child and lying all night upon the ground (II Samuel 12:16). When, despite the fast, the child died, David 'arose from the earth and washed and anointed himself and changed his clothes' (II Samuel 12:20). After the exile, the official fasts were accompanied by special readings from the scripture. Six further benedictions were added to the normal eighteen of the Amidah prayer and the liturgy was supplemented by special penitential prayers and dirges. The people tore their garments as a sign of mourning; they wore sackcloth and they put ashes on their heads. The ritual objects also shared in the humiliation. The Ark was draped in white or even in sackcloth and all superfluous decoration was removed. In these early days the people assembled together and were rebuked for their failings. Everyone was expected to refrain from eating, although exceptions were made for young children, animals, pregnant and nursing mothers and the sick.

Ordinary fast days lasted during the hours of daylight, but the important fasts, the Day of Atonement and the ninth day of Av, began at sunset on the previous day and continued until the following nightfall. In the first century CE, Hananiah ben Hezekiah ben Garon formulated a Scroll of Fasting which lists thirty-five dates on which fasts should not be proclaimed. Presumably, by that stage, fasts were becoming so common that they were beginning to infringe on Sabbaths and festivals. After the destruction of the Second Temple by the Romans in CE 70, individuals took it upon themselves to fast on every Monday and every Thursday as a sign of mourning. According to the

Talmud, the minor fasts must be observed with full rigour during times of trial and persecution. The prophet Zechariah, on the other hand, makes it clear that once the Messiah comes, there will be no more fasting and the days of mourning will become times of joy and gladness (18:19). The question then arose as to what should be done in the intermediate times. Eventually it was decided that they should be daytime rather than twenty-four-hour fasts. Once the State of Israel had been founded, the question arose as to whether any fasting was still appropriate. This was a real problem. The return of the exiles to the Promised Land was supposed to be an event of the messianic era. If so, then the creation of the State of Israel was the start of the days of the Messiah and fasting should be abolished. Most Orthodox authorities, however, did not reach that conclusion and the fasts continue to be strictly observed.

Elements of fasting include abstention from food and drink. It is said that going hungry, even for a single day, encourages sympathy for the poor and oppressed. In addition, bathing (except for the fingers and eyes) and anointing the body with oil are forbidden. The pious Jew may not make love, and 'putting on sandals' is not allowed. This last has been interpreted as not wearing leather shoes. A possible explanation for this is that leather is obtained from slaughtered animals. On the day on which humankind asks God for mercy, it is not right to be merciless to God's creatures. In general, Judaism is not a particularly ascetic religion but, through the regular pattern of fasts, the worshippers can discipline their physical natures and vicariously share in the disasters that have befallen the Jewish people through the ages.

10
Childhood and youth

Birth ceremonies

The first commandment in the Hebrew scriptures was given to
Adam and Eve, the first human beings; it was to be fruitful and
multiply (Genesis 1:28). Having children is an important
element in the Jewish tradition. Religious life is centred around
the home as well as the synagogue and there is a strong feeling
that the tradition must be handed down from generation to
generation. Arguably an important component in the crisis of
the community today is the current trend of delaying marriage
or choosing an alternative lifestyle. Many people are remaining
single until their thirties and enjoying a high standard of living;
the birth-rate is consequently low. New households are not
being formed and children are not being born. In the past,
however, a large family was regarded as a blessing and life
centred around the rearing of offspring. To live to a good age
and to be the patriarch or matriarch of a large clan was everyone's ultimate desire.

According to traditional law, a woman was considered to be
ritually unclean for seven days after giving birth to a boy and for
fourteen days after giving birth to a girl. Subsequently she was
not allowed to enter the Temple precincts for thirty-three days
(for a boy) or sixty-six (for a girl). The Strictly Orthodox still
keep the laws of purity and a woman is forbidden to her husband
for these periods. The non-Orthodox have abandoned these
practices as archaic and discriminatory towards women. Jewish

law, nonetheless, is unequivocal that the life of the mother takes precedence over the life of an unborn baby, whether boy or girl. Only when the child is more than halfway emerged from the birth canal is it considered to be a full human being with human rights. Thus, although abortion is considered to be a serious offence, it is not regarded as infanticide and even the most Orthodox Jews are less strict in this matter than are their Roman Catholic counterparts.

In the past, the birth of a child was accompanied by an array of superstitions. Amulets were hung near the sleeping baby to ward off evil spirits, and family and friends would gather together regularly to pray for the protection of the new arrival. In particular, Lilith, the queen of the demons, was most feared. According to legend, she was the first wife of Adam and, like him, was created from the dust of the ground. She refused to be an obedient wife and, in consequence, she was cast out and God created Eve from Adam's rib in her place. Lilith was said to have designs on new-born babies and her influence was much feared. It is one of the paradoxes of modern Jewish life that Lilith has in recent years been adopted as a heroine, and a Jewish feminist magazine has been named in her honour!

Among German Jews it was the custom to swaddle infants. The strip of linen that was used to bind a little boy was carefully kept. Later it was embroidered and, at the boy's bar mitzvah ceremony, when the lad reached the age of thirteen, it was presented to the synagogue as a Torah binder. It was also the custom for new mothers to visit the synagogue soon after the birth to recite a blessing expressing gratitude to God. The child was named either at the circumcision service (for boys) or at a baby blessing (for girls) in the synagogue. Every Jew is given a Hebrew name. Traditionally among the Ashkenazim (Eastern Europeans), the child is named after a relative who has recently died; among the Sephardim (Orientals) the name of a living relation is chosen. The new name is coupled with the name of his or her father – so a boy might be Jacob ben (son of) Isaac and a girl would be Dinah bat (daughter of) Jacob. This Hebrew name is put on all formal religious documents and is used when an individual is called up to read from the Torah scroll in the synagogue. For everyday life it is frequently secularized – so Jacob could become James and Dinah Diana.

The first time the Torah is read in the synagogue after the birth of a little girl, the father is called up in honour of the new baby. This can well occur on a weekday when there are barely ten men in the building. Compared with the fanfare accompanying a circumcision, it can scarcely be described as a celebration. There is no doubt that Judaism is a patriarchal tradition. Modern Orthodox authorities may try to explain away these anomalies in deference to feminine feelings, but there is no escaping the essential sexism of the liturgy. Every day in the synagogue, men actually give praise to God. 'Blessed art Thou, O Lord our God, who hast not made me a woman.'[1]

Circumcision

According to Jewish law, all male children must be circumcised. This is believed to go back to the time of the first Jew, Abraham. In the book of Genesis, God commanded: 'This is My covenant which you shall keep, between Me and you and your descendants after you: Every male among you shall be circumcised ... and it shall be a sign of the covenant between Me and you. ... He that is eight days old among you shall be circumcised, every male throughout your generations' (17:10–12). There is a story that a Roman governor of the Holy Land asked Rabbi Akiva (second century CE) why circumcision was necessary. If God did not want a man to have a foreskin, why did He create him with one? Akiva replied that God had created an incomplete and imperfect world and it was up to man to make it complete and perfect.

The operation is still performed on the eighth day after the birth, and can take place on the Sabbath, on festivals and even on the Day of Atonement. However, if there is any indication that the child is not yet healthy enough for the procedure, it can be delayed. It is important to emphasize that circumcision does not make the baby a Jew; he is a Jew anyway by virtue of his having been born of a Jewish mother. Rather, it is a sign that he is a member of the covenant. Male converts to Judaism must also be circumcised and, if a Jewish man was not circumcised as an infant, he should be circumcised as an adult. In Hebrew the operation is described as *berit milah*, literally the covenant of circumcision. So fundamental is it to Jewish identity that the ceremony is simply described as 'the brit'.

In the early days of the Reform movement, some of the Reformers moved to have the rite abolished. One of their leading spokesmen, Abraham Geiger (1810–76), privately described it as 'a barbaric, bloody act which fills the father with fear'. In the secular world, the fashion for circumcision waxes and wanes. For many years in the twentieth century, a large proportion of all baby boys was circumcised as a matter of course. Today, however, many medical authorities consider that, in general, it is better if the baby is not circumcised, as the procedure is traumatic. Nonetheless, even the most assimilated and secular Jews continue to circumcise their sons. The compromise in this case tends to be that the operation is done by a surgeon in a hospital with no accompanying religious rite.

The orthodox religious ceremony can be done at home or in a private room in the synagogue during the course of the morning service. The baby is handed by a godmother to a godfather and on to the *sandak*, who is responsible for holding him on his knee while the operation takes place. The godparents may simply be friends of the parents; often they are an engaged or even a childless couple who, by performing this service, may be enabled to have children of their own. The *sandak* is generally one of the grandfathers or another eminent member of the community. The operation itself is performed by a *mohel*, a professional circumciser. This is a job that requires considerable training; the law permits any Jewish doctor to do a circumcision, but, in the event, most doctors prefer to leave it to a trained and experienced *mohel*. Once the baby is securely on the knee of the *sandak*, the father makes the blessing, 'Blessed art Thou, O Lord our God, King of the Universe, who hast sanctified us with Thy commandments and hast commanded us to make our sons enter the covenant of Abraham.' To this, the rest of the gathering responds, 'Even as this child has entered into the covenant, so may he enter into the Torah, the marriage canopy and into good deeds.' After the operation is completed, the *mohel* recites a prayer for the baby over a cup of wine and gives him his Hebrew name. The child is given a few drops of wine and afterwards there is a celebratory meal. This includes a grace after the meal in which the parents, the infant, the *mohel* and the *sandak* are all blessed. It is a tremendous occasion. Grandparents and relatives will travel long distances to be there and there is much rejoicing.

In recent years there have been attempts to devise a service for baby girls, celebrating their entry into the covenant. Various alternatives have been proposed, but none has succeeded in providing a similar potent mix of pain, insecurity, blood, family solidarity and ancient symbolism. The fact remains that the birth of a boy produces a greater occasion for celebration than the birth of a girl. Still greater is the jollification if the little boy is the first-born of his mother.

The redemption of the first-born

According to the Hebrew scriptures, 'The Lord said to Moses: Consecrate to Me all the first-born; whatever is the first to open the womb among the people of Israel, both of man and beast, is Mine' (Exodus 13:1–2). Similarly, in the book of Numbers:

> Everything that opens the womb of all flesh, whether man or beast, which they offer to the Lord shall be yours [Aaron's, the ancestor of the priests]; nevertheless the first-born of man you shall redeem ... And their redemption price – at a month old you shall redeem them – you shall fix at five shekels in silver, according to the shekels of the sanctuary which is twenty gerahs. (18:15–16)

This is understood to mean that every first child who happens to be male must be formally redeemed from a priest. If the mother already has a daughter or if she has had an earlier miscarriage or an abortion, then the law no longer applies. On the other hand, if a widower who already has children marries a young woman and her first child is a boy, then the father must redeem the child, even if he has already redeemed another older son. The ceremony takes place when the infant is thirty-one days old and it is one of the few occasions when there is an official role for a priest in Judaism. In the days of the Temple, the descendants of Aaron, the brother of Moses, served as priests. Once the Temple was destroyed in CE 70, their function largely disappeared. However, the knowledge of Aaronic descent was passed down from father to son to this day. There is no documentary evidence so the family legend may or may not be accurate. The term for priest in Hebrew is *kohen* and, in general, most families whose surname is Cohen or Kohen claim priestly ancestry.

During the ceremony the baby is formally brought into the room – sometimes on a silver platter – and the father gives him to the priest. He then makes the declaration, 'This is my first-born, the first-born of his mother and the Holy One, Blessed be He, has given the commandment to redeem him.' The father then puts down the sum of five silver shekels in front of the priest. Today there is some doubt as to the modern equivalent of shekels and the convention is that some article, such as a candlestick, containing at least 96 grams of silver is adequate, but in fact any relatively valuable object will do. The priest then gives the father a choice. He asks, 'Which would you rather, give me your first-born son, the first-born of his mother, or redeem him for five shekels, which you are bound to give according to the Torah.' The joke is frequently made that after a month of sleepless nights with a crying baby, the father might prefer to keep the silver, but the liturgy determines otherwise. He replies, 'I desire rather to redeem my son and here you have the value of his redemption, which I am bound to give you according to the Torah.' The child is returned to his father and the father recites the benedictions, 'Blessed art Thou, O Lord our God, King of the Universe, who hast sanctified us by Thy commandments and commanded us according to the redemption of the first-born' and 'Blessed art Thou, O Lord our God, King of the Universe, who hast kept us in life, hast preserved us and hast enabled us to reach this season.' The priest holds the silver over the baby and says, 'This instead of that, this is in commutation for that and this is in remission for that.' He then prays for the child and gives the priestly benediction. Traditionally the ceremony is followed by a party. The priest is entitled to keep the silver, but in fact he often chooses to donate the object to charity or he simply returns it to the father.

The leaders of the Reform movement have abandoned this tradition. Firstly they are not convinced by claims of priestly ancestry and secondly they perceive it to be discriminatory to girl babies. The ceremony also does not take place if the father himself is a priest or if the mother is the daughter of a priest, because in that instance the priests already have the baby. A *pidyon-ha-ben*, as the Redemption is called in Hebrew, is invariably a delightful affair and it must encourage every Orthodox young woman to hope that her first-born will be a son.

Elementary and secondary education

According to Jewish law, parents have an obligation to educate their children. In the book of Deuteronomy, God said of His commandments, 'You shall teach them diligently to your children, and shall talk of them when you sit in your house and when you walk by the way and when you sit down and when you rise' (6:7). The emphasis is on passing down the tradition through the generations:

> When your son asks you in time to come: What is the meaning
> of the testimonies and statutes and the ordinances which the
> Lord God has commanded you? Then you shall say to your son:
> We were Pharaoh's slaves in Egypt, and the Lord brought us
> out of Egypt with a mighty hand ... And the Lord commanded
> us to do all these statutes. (Deuteronomy 6:20–21, 24)

The education of children has been a fundamental priority for the community from earliest times. The book of Proverbs makes its importance clear: 'Train up a child in the way he should go, and when he is old he will not depart from it' (22:6); 'A wise son hears his father's instruction' (13:1); and 'He who spares the rod hates his son, but he who loves him is diligent to discipline him' (13:24). In the Mishnah, the sages described the appropriate ages for study: 'Five years old is the age for the study of the Bible, ten years old for the Mishnah; at thirteen the child is obliged to keep the commandments and at fifteen it is time for him to start on the Talmud.'[2]

In the Orthodox world, this pattern is still largely followed. Often, the first time a small boy is sat down to study, he will find a sweetmeat in the pages of the book – to encourage him to see Torah study as sweet and pleasant. Children are sent to Jewish elementary schools where extensive religious, as well as ordinary secular knowledge, is part of the curriculum. In such schools, by the age of seven, the children are expected to read both Hebrew and the language of their country. They study passages from the Bible from an early age and they learn about the Jewish way of life both at school and from living it at home. These schools have grown out of the traditional one-room elementary schools of Eastern Europe. There the small boys of the village learned Hebrew and Bible. Since there has been almost universal literacy among Hebrew men for centuries, teaching was not a prestigious job, as it was felt that anyone could do it. Today, however, Jewish elementary day schools are highly professional operations. They have to be certified by the secular government; they are generally well equipped and, in spite of the emphasis on Jewish studies, the children seem to do as well in their secular subjects as do their non-Jewish counterparts in ordinary schools. In addition, they are for girls as well as boys, even though, in very Orthodox establishments, the sexes are taught separately.

Outside the Orthodox community, most Jewish parents do not want this type of education for their children. In recent years both the Conservative and Reform movements have set up their own schools, but the majority of Jewish children today go to secular schools. For them, synagogues organize a system of supplementary Jewish studies and the children attend classes after school and on Sundays. The quality of teaching varies and the enterprise is all too often bedevilled by the children's perception that it is secular schooling that 'really matters'. Nonetheless enormous efforts are made in these supplementary schools to provide an introduction to and an experience of the Jewish tradition. Classes may begin at the pre-school level and the students are encouraged to stay until the age of at least sixteen. For those who complete the course, graduation is celebrated in the synagogue with a confirmation service conducted by the young people themselves, and often the synagogue will organize a youth trip to Israel as a reward for finishing.

This supplementary Jewish education is regarded as totally inadequate by the Strictly Orthodox. Their sons, at the age of fourteen, move from elementary school to a Jewish high school. There, while following a normal secondary schooling course, they also concentrate on studying the Mishnah, the Talmud and *musar* (ethics). It is a thorough initiation, designed as a preparation for a lifetime of study. Parallel secondary schools for girls were not set up until the early years of the twentieth century. Instead, girls learnt the domestic arts at home and waited for marriage. Today, however, the Beth Jacob high schools provide four years of Jewish and secular education from the ages of fourteen to eighteen. The girls, however, follow a different curriculum from that of their brothers since the Strictly Orthodox do not encourage women to study Talmud. However, the vast majority of Jewish children do not enjoy such an intensive religious education. For them, the crown of their achievement in this department is demonstrated at their coming of age ceremony, their bar or bat mitzvah.

Bar and bat mitzvah

At the age of thirteen, a boy attains Jewish adulthood. From then on, he is expected to keep the commandments and his presence in the synagogue counts towards the necessary quorum for worship. The term *bar mitzvah* means literally 'son of commandment' and, from the Middle Ages, attaining this status was a cause for celebration. The essential of the bar mitzvah ceremony involved being called up to read from the Torah scroll in the synagogue.

Different communities followed different practices. In Eastern Europe, it was usual for the boy to be called up to the Torah scroll on the first Monday or Thursday after his birthday. He would recite the Torah blessings and chant some verses from the weekly reading. In Western Europe, the tradition was that the service took place on the Sabbath and the boy read from the set prophetic reading as well as from the Torah. Usually he would also give a speech in which he demonstrated his knowledge of rabbinic sources and the father would recite a special blessing. The service would then be followed by a small party for the community.

The bar mitzvah service is not a big ordeal for a child who has had a traditional Jewish education. He can already read Hebrew fluently and he understands what he reads. The Torah scroll is harder to decipher than the printed text of the Bible because it is written without vowels, but nonetheless the words and the stories are very familiar. For the child without this sort of background, it is far harder. Often he is a complete beginner in Hebrew reading and he has to start with the alphabet. Generally, even with intensive coaching, all that can be expected is that the boy learns to read the text fluently. He will know what the passage means, but he would not be able to translate it for himself.

More seriously, the bar mitzvah has all too often become an occasion for lavish one-upmanship. Parents are willing to spend extraordinary sums of money. Friends and relations come from afar to stay for the weekend. They may be housed in an expensive hotel and there may be pre-bar mitzvah dinners and post-bar mitzvah outings. The reception after the ceremony may be a most grandiose party with professional entertainers and a special theme (baseball? circuses? motor racing?) which has nothing to do with Judaism. Every guest is expected to bring a gift, and the lad can find himself surrounded by innumerable watches, pocket knives, articles of clothing and sporting equipment. It is not unknown for boys partially to finance their college education from the cheques given at the bar mitzvah.

It must be stressed that not all bar mitzvahs are like this. Some families make the decision that, come what may, they will do it very simply – for example just the ceremony followed by cake and wine for the congregation afterwards. But community pressure may be too great. In general, the religious establishment is very embarrassed by the excesses, but feels powerless to stop them. Even more disappointingly, once the bar mitzvah celebrations come to an end, the child feels no incentive to continue with his Jewish education. All too often, with the full support of his parents, he drops out of supplementary religion school.

In order to counter these undesirable trends, the Reform movement initially abolished the bar mitzvah. The Reformers hoped to keep both boys and girls in religion school, by introducing a ceremony of group confirmation at the age of sixteen. It did not work. Parents wanted to throw the party, to enjoy the community recognition and to watch with pride their sons reading in the synagogue. However, they were well aware that the situation discriminated against girls and this could not be allowed to continue.

In the tradition, girls are regarded as having reached religious maturity at the age of twelve, but there is no legal obligation for the occasion to be marked in any special way. Among the Strictly Orthodox, little has changed. Twelve may be regarded as a special birthday, but there is no religious celebration. However, twentieth-century attitudes have prevailed in the other segments of the community. Among the non-Orthodox, the bat mitzvah (as it is called) can be identical in every way to the bar mitzvah. Among the modern Orthodox, there are still reservations about a girl reading from the Torah scroll in public, but she still may conduct prayers and chant the prophetic reading. Alternatively, some Orthodox communities conduct a collective service for all the twelve-year-old girls each year. In any event, most Jewish girls today can expect some formal recognition that they have reached the age of maturity.

11
Maturity

Higher education

For the Strictly Orthodox, religious education certainly does not end with the bar mitzvah. Four years of Jewish high school follow which combine secular and Jewish studies. Then the young man will probably go off to yeshiva for several years. Ayeshiva (plural yeshivot) is an academy dedicated to the study of the Talmud and the other sacred texts. Academies of higher learning were established in both the Holy Land and in Babylonia as early as in the first century CE. These establishments kept in contact with one another and attracted students from all over the Jewish world. Particularly famous was the academy founded by Johanan ben Zakkai (first century) in Jabneh after the destruction of Jerusalem in CE 70. The academies of Sura and Pumbedita were founded in Babylonia in the third century and also exerted an enormous influence. Individual scholars were known as Rabbi (in the Holy Land) and as Rav (in Babylon) and, arguably, Judaism owes its very survival to the efforts of these leaders.

In the nineteenth century, yeshivot were organized throughout Eastern Europe; the establishments at Tels, Ponovezh and Slobodka and the Hasidic schools at Lubavitch and Lublin were among the best known. These were all destroyed in the Nazi Holocaust. After the war, new yeshivot were set up in the United States, in Israel and in Europe. Today there are more yeshiva students than at any other time in history. This is not the result of an increase in the Jewish population – in fact, world Jewry has shrunk. It is the consequence of increased affluence.

In the past only a few could afford to continue their education beyond the age of fourteen or sixteen. They had to work to contribute to the family income. Today almost every young man from a Strictly Orthodox background expects to have the opportunity of yeshiva study.

Most yeshivot are organized along the traditional Lithuanian lines. The students work, generally in pairs, in a large hall and together they argue out the meaning of the sacred texts. The debate is conducted in Yiddish as they pore over the Aramaic writing. Twice a week, the head of the yeshiva will give a lecture on the portion of the Talmud that is being studied. There is also a moral tutor who gives regular talks on *musar* (ethics). The students are largely expected to work on their own and the full course lasts four years. It does not necessarily lead to a career in the practical rabbinate; the majority of graduates eventually earn their living in secular occupations. However, almost every yeshiva has a *kolel*, an advanced section, in which married students and their families are supported as they continue their studies still further. This may lead to a rabbinical career.

The Yeshiva world, as it is called, has become immensely influential, particularly in Israel. Members are staunch upholders of the Orthodox traditions. They are tireless campaigners for such issues as the closure of roads on the Sabbath and the changing of the Law of Return to exclude Reform converts. However, the Strictly Orthodox do not have a monopoly on Jewish higher education. In the nineteenth century, non-Orthodox rabbinical seminaries were founded in the United States. The Hebrew Union College (Reform) was established in Cincinnati, Ohio, in 1875. It was modelled on the Reform seminary in Berlin and today it also has branches in New York, Los Angeles and Jerusalem. Soon afterwards, the Jewish Theological Seminary (Conservative) was founded in New York. After World War II, the Leo Baeck College was set up in

London to train non-Orthodox rabbis for Europe and the British Commonwealth. New York's Yeshiva University was founded on neo-Orthodox principles together with its companion institution, Stern College for Women. Eventually all these seminaries developed graduate schools in a wide range of fields. Not only do they ordain rabbis, they also train social workers and teachers of Jewish studies; they train cantors in their schools of sacred music and they award masters' degrees and doctorates in biblical, rabbinic, historical and theological subjects.

The vast majority of Jewish young people, however, are not religious scholars. They concentrate on their secular studies. Today it is rare for a Jewish boy or girl to leave school at the minimum leaving age. Jewish parents are anxious that all their children should achieve their full academic potential. The traditional Jewish commitment to education has been translated into a determination that their young should attend prestigious universities and attain the highest possible professional qualifications. Today the old joke 'my son the doctor' is just as likely to be 'my daughter the lawyer' or even 'my twins the professors'. Today the proportion of Jewish young people in higher education exceeds many times over their proportion in the population as a whole.

Courtship and marriage

Judaism does not have a tradition of celibacy. According to the story in the book of Genesis, when God first created man, He pronounced, 'It is not good for the man to be alone.' Therefore He created the first woman and He 'brought her to the man. And the man said: This at last is bone of my bone and flesh and of my flesh . . . Therefore a man leaves his father and his mother and cleaves to his wife, and they become one flesh' (2:18, 22–3). Apart from the Essenes, a desert sect of the first centuries

BCE/CE, there have been no Jewish celibate communities. A story is told of one Simeon ben Azzal (second century CE) who used to preach sermons on the duty of procreation while firmly remaining single himself. He used to argue that he himself was in love with the Torah. But his stance was exceptional; Jews are expected to marry.

Today, the only sector of the community that seems to have no difficulty with this is the Strictly Orthodox. Here early marriage remains the norm. Boys and girls are educated separately, and they are largely kept apart through adolescence. Then, during the young man's final years at yeshiva, he is expected to get married, and families, friends and teachers are all co-opted to find a suitable bride. In the old days, in the villages of Eastern Europe, there was a recognized matchmaker who organized the brokering between the families and who made the introductions. Today it is more informal, and it is not true to say that marriages are exactly arranged. Nonetheless, anxious parents keep a close eye on proceedings. The process was described to the authors by one mother who had already succeeded in marrying off three daughters, all in their very early twenties: 'We try to check out the boy to see if things match each other. You always know somebody who knows somebody who knows somebody. So basically we called up and checked up on the school and the synagogue and the rabbi and so on. There were times that I called up and I didn't like what I heard. There's no point in her going out with somebody if it's not going to work out ... so I said "No" and she herself did not want to go out with this one.' It is quite usual for the boy still to be a student when he marries; the couple are financed by both sets of parents until the young husband is ready to take on the duty of supporting his family.

Things are not so straightforward elsewhere in the community. Most Jewish children go to secular, coeducational schools. They attend secular universities and they often travel far from home to complete their education and for their first job. Parents have far less control. According to Jewish law, certain marriages have no validity – in particular those that are incestuous (such as between father and daughter or brother and sister), those that are adulterous (when one partner is already married to someone else) and those between a Jew and a gentile. It is this last that is the greatest threat. In the past when Jews were isolated in their own communities or when there was serious anti-Semitism, the danger of intermarriage was small. Today in the State of Israel, for obvious reasons, Jews are likely to marry Jews. In the Dispersion, it is a different story. Young Jewish men and women who have studied at prestigious universities and have entered the learned professions are highly desirable marriage partners by any standard. All too often they 'marry out'.

The religious establishment does its best to combat the tendency. Part of the drive behind the creation of non-Orthodox Jewish day schools is to help children grow up in a more Jewish milieu. Children are sent to Jewish summer camps; there are university Jewish societies and in every city the community organizes an array of singles events. There is also considerable pressure from parents. In the past, if a child married a gentile, he or she was often cut off from the family for ever. Today this is well-nigh inconceivable; almost every family is touched by intermarriage and the community seems powerless to stop it. Today in the United States, more than 50 per cent of marriages involving Jews are mixed marriages.

In fact, this is only one aspect of the problem of marriage. Jews, in common with most well-educated young people, tend to marry late. Many neglect to get married at all. Perhaps they are homosexual, perhaps they are happier to live by themselves, perhaps they have had a bad early experience or perhaps they simply leave it for too long. In any event non-marriage and intermarriage are perceived to be the greatest problems facing the Jewish community today. Indeed, it has been calculated that if present trend continues, only the strictly Orthodox communities will be left in the Dispersion by the end of the twenty-first century. It is a frightening prospect.

The marriage ceremony

Let us imagine that the prayers of friends and relatives are answered. Some time during his late twenties, the son of the household meets a Jewish girl and they fall in love. To the delight of both families, they announce that they want to be married. The rabbi is informed, the synagogue or other venue is booked and the caterers are engaged. There is going to be a Jewish wedding.

In biblical and talmudic times, weddings took place in two stages. The first element was the betrothal. This involved the delivery of an object of monetary value by the bridegroom to the bride in front of two witnesses. The object (which is now invariably a wedding ring) was given with the words, 'Behold, you are consecrated to me with this ring, according to the law of Moses and Israel.' Then the blessing over the wine was recited. The bride continued to live in her father's house and the couple were not regarded as married. Nonetheless, a contract existed between them which could only be dissolved by a formal divorce. The second stage was the wedding proper. This involved the young couple standing together under the marriage canopy. The marriage contract, the *ketubah*, was drawn up and the marriage benedictions were recited in front of a religious quorum of at least ten adult men. Then they were married; they were free to live together and could establish their own home. Since the Middle Ages, however, the two stages have been combined and the betrothal and wedding ceremonies take place one after the other.

The normal course of proceedings is as follows: first the marriage contract must be signed. This document dates from talmudic times and is written in Aramaic (the language of the Talmud). It settles a sum of money on the wife which the husband is obliged to pay in the event of a divorce. This was intended to offer a measure of protection to the woman. Today, of course, marriages are subject to the laws of the land, so the document is a formality. It is still an essential part of any Jewish wedding and it is frequently a beautifully illuminated document which can be hung with pride in the new home.

After the contract is signed, the bride and groom, together with both sets of parents, all stand together under the *huppah* or marriage canopy. The canopy symbolizes the Jewish home and has become synonymous with the wedding ceremony, so that at a circumcision the parents pray that they may have the joy of escorting their child to the canopy. Psalms are recited and then the rabbi often gives a short address. He takes a cup of wine and recites first the benediction over the wine and then the benediction over the betrothal, 'Blessed art Thou, O Lord, who hast hallowed Thy people Israel by the rite of the wedding canopy and the sacred covenant of marriage.' Both bride and groom drink from the cup and the bridegroom puts the wedding ring on the bride's finger with the traditional betrothal words of consecration.

This is followed by the seven benedictions in which blessings are asked for the young couple over a second cup of wine. The ceremony concludes with the bridegroom stamping on a glass and breaking it. The origin of this custom is obscure, but it is thought to be a reminder that even during the joy of a wedding, the destruction of Jerusalem must be remembered. At this all the congregation say '*Mazal tov*', meaning good luck. Weddings are supremely happy occasions in the Jewish tradition. It is thought that the union between husband and wife reflects the union between the emanations of God; it is a recreation of the ultimate harmony of the universe and, to quote one of the benedictions, it is a state of 'joy and gladness, laughter and exultation, pleasure and delight, love, peace and friendship'.

Different communities have different wedding customs. Today in the West, weddings generally include the paraphernalia of a best man, ushers and bridesmaids. Among the Strictly Orthodox, the groom fasts all day and, after he has signed the contract, he is taken to see the bride and he covers her face with a veil. Then the parents lead the young couple to the canopy in a procession of lighted candles. In Oriental communities, a special celebration for the bride takes place on the evening before the wedding. The bride has already immersed herself in the ritual bath. Then, at home, female family and friends paint her hands with red henna and dress her in splendid clothes. Among the non-Orthodox, there are attempts to make the service more egalitarian with two rings and the bride as well as the bridegroom reciting blessings. In any event, the core of the ceremony remains. Jewish marriage is characterized by the contract, the canopy, the giving of the ring and the public declaration in front of witnesses.

The laws of family purity

It has already been mentioned that an Orthodox bride will visit the ritual bath (the *mikveh*) before her wedding. A ritual bath is a pool like a very small swimming pool. According to the provisions of the Talmud, it must be supplied partially by a spring or a tank of rain water. This is because the book of Leviticus declares that 'a spring or a cistern holding waters shall be clean' (11:36). The rabbis interpreted this to mean that ritual contamination can be cleansed but the water must not be poured from another container. It must come directly from nature. This 'natural' water can subsequently be mixed with other waters (from the tap) to make the whole into an agent of cleanliness.

The ritual bath is used by a few, very pious Jewish men before the Day of Atonement. They immerse themselves in preparation for this most holy of days. Among the Hasidim, the bath may be used weekly just before the Sabbath or even daily before prayer. Ritual immersion is also an important element in the traditional conversion ceremony by which non-Jews are received into Judaism. However, even among the Orthodox, the people who use the ritual bath most are pre-menopausal married women.

According to Jewish law, husbands and wives may not have sexual relations during the days of the wife's monthly period, nor for seven clear days afterwards. This means that among the Orthodox the wedding date is calculated to fit in with the bride's menstrual flow so that she is married during her 'clean period'. During the time that she is forbidden to her husband, the couple sleep in separate beds and avoid touching each other in any way at all. (This is why Strictly Orthodox men will avoid even shaking hands with women.) Then, after the flow has ended and seven full days have elapsed, the wife visits the ritual bath.

A modern ritual bath has the feminine, matter-of-fact feel of a provincial beauty parlour. It is presided over by a pious, respected woman of the community and it is traditional to visit privately in the evening. Before immersion, the woman must have a very thorough wash. For the immersion to be valid, every inch of the surface of her body must come into contact with the ritual waters, so all trace of dirt must be removed. Finger- and toenails are trimmed and the hair is thoroughly combed out. Among the Strictly Orthodox, it is the practice for a married woman to cut off her hair and wear a wig. This has the double benefit of fulfilling the commandment that married women must cover their hair and it makes the monthly visit to the ritual bath easier to manage. When the supervisor is satisfied that the woman is completely clean and her hair free from tangles, she is directed to the ritual bath itself. There she immerses herself completely so that the waters cover her head, and she recites the traditional blessings. Then she can resume marital relations with her husband.

Traditionally the duty of building a ritual bath outweighs even the duty of building a synagogue. Today, however, there are many more synagogues than ritual baths – implying that only the Orthodox keep the laws of family purity. They are certainly not easy. Even if a woman's periods are strictly regular, she and her husband are forbidden to make love for at least twelve days out of every twenty-eight. Those who follow the laws argue that they keep the marriage fresh and that each time the husband and wife come together again, it is like a honeymoon. It is also maintained, but on little scientific basis, that these laws protect a woman against cervical cancer. What is certain is that the couple resume sexual relations during what is likely to be the wife's most fertile period.

Attitudes to artificial birth-control within the Jewish tradition are not entirely clear. On the one hand, it is the duty of every couple to procreate, and sexual pleasure within marriage is regarded as a positive good. In view of this it is perhaps surprising that Orthodox families are not even larger! On the other hand, the life of the mother must be protected at all costs, and some authorities argue that duty is done when the marriage has produced one son and one daughter. In view of this, it does seem probable that modern birth-control methods are used on occasion. Certainly female devices are regarded with less disapproval than male methods since it is important to avoid the sin described in the Talmud as 'wasting seed'. Among the non-Orthodox, of course, none of these considerations apply. Both Reform and secular Jews tend to reject the laws of family purity as both primitive and discriminatory to women and they certainly take advantage of modern contraceptive methods.

Divorce

The Jewish tradition recognizes that marriages sometimes break down. This is not to say that divorce is to be encouraged; in fact, it is regarded as a tragedy and, according to the Talmud, the very altar of God weeps when a man divorces his wife. Nonetheless divorce is regarded as an occasional and sad necessity and formal procedures are laid down in the law. The book of Deuteronomy gives a brief outline of what happens: 'When a man takes a wife and marries her, if she finds no favour in his eyes because he has found some indecency in her, he writes a bill of divorce and puts it in her hand and sends her out of his house' (24:1).

In ancient times men, but not women, were allowed to have more than one spouse. The woman was consecrated wholly to the man, but the man could have several commitments. If a man was tired of his wife, he could always take another, but this option was not open to women. If she took another man, the relationship was adulterous and any subsequent child was regarded as a *mamzer* (ritual bastard) who faced a major ritual disability. A *mamzer* could only marry another *mamzer* and his or her children inherited the status 'unto ten generations'. This terrible state of affairs was to be avoided at all costs and it was done by giving the woman a formal bill of divorce in front of witnesses.

Although polygamy has been outlawed among Eastern European Jews since the eleventh century, the law still requires a man who wants to be rid of his wife to give her a proper divorce. It is not so important for men since adultery is defined as a carnal relationship with a married woman. It is wrong for an undivorced man to set up house with another unmarried woman, but their children will not have the *mamzer* status.

A man may not divorce his wife for no reason at all, and in any event the woman is protected by her marriage document. The bride price must be returned before a divorce can be granted. Today, the normal procedure outside Israel is to wait until the couple are divorced civilly. Then the husband and wife attend a meeting of the religious court. There the bill of divorce is written out in Aramaic by a special scribe. After the document has been read and signed by the two witnesses, the husband formally delivers it into the wife's hands. In the state of Israel, this is the only procedure by which a Jewish couple may get divorced.

In the past, when Jews lived together in small closed communities, difficulties only arose if the husband disappeared, went missing in battle or was lost at sea with no witnesses. If a woman found herself married to an intolerable man, the community could put pressure on the husband to give her a divorce. In an extreme case a ban might be put on the husband so no one had anything to do with him. Eventually social and economic isolation would compel him to submit.

Today in the Dispersion there is a real problem. If a husband refuses to grant his wife a religious divorce, there is very little that can be done about it. The wife finds herself in an impossible position. Her status is that of an *agunah*, a tied woman. She is unable to marry again and she is stuck in limbo, neither married nor divorced. She is compelled to live by herself and is a source of embarrassment to herself and to the community. All too often the religious divorce is used as a blackmailing tool to compel the wife to accept a less-than-equitable financial settlement and the woman is powerless to defend herself. Admittedly the husband cannot marry another Jewish woman, but in some cases he does not care or his hatred of his wife is so great that he will put up with this inconvenience to get back at her. In any event, it is a real imbalance in the powers of men and women.

The Reform movement has solved the problem by regarding a civil divorce as tantamount to a religious divorce. This appalls the Orthodox because it means, particularly in America, that thousands of *mamzerim* are being born as a result of second marriages. Various suggestions have been made within the Orthodox establishment to solve the problem of the 'tied woman', but either the will or the legal ingenuity is lacking. Meanwhile far too many women face life on their own, their freedom dependent on the whim of the men they were once unfortunate enough to marry.

12

The Jewish home and everyday living

Phylacteries and Mezuzah

The Orthodox Jew says the Shema prayer every day, both when he rises in the morning and when he goes to bed at night. It contains the reminder that God's words, His Torah, should be bound 'as a sign upon your hand and they shall be as frontlets between your eyes. And you shall write them on the doorposts of your house and on your gates' (Deuteronomy 6:8–9). For generations the Jewish community has understood these words as referring to the duties of putting on phylacteries and nailing a mezuzah to the doorpost.

Phylacteries are special boxes containing biblical verses written by hand on parchment. The verses are Exodus 13:1–10 (on the laws relating to the dedication of the first-born to God's service), Exodus 13:11–16 (repeating the laws of the first-born and the commandment to teach children about the miraculous deliverance from slavery in Egypt), Deuteronomy 6:4–9 (the first paragraph of the Shema prayer stressing the oneness of God) and Deuteronomy 11:13–21 (the second paragraph of the Shema prayer on reward and punishment). The boxes are attached to straps. One is placed over the head so that the box sits squarely upon the forehead between the eyes. The other is wound round the left arm so that the box faces the heart. The strap is placed in a special way so that it forms the Hebrew letter shin, the first letter of God's name *El Shaddai* – God Almighty.

The Hebrew word for phylacteries is *tephillin*, and the action of putting on the boxes is known as laying tephillin. It is an ancient practice and is even mentioned in the New Testament. Jesus accused the Pharisees of his time of loving to make their phylacteries broad and their fringes long (Matthew 23:5). It should be observed by all male Jews of bar mitzvah age and above and is performed every weekday either at home or in the synagogue. Phylacteries are not put on on the Sabbath or on festivals. Among the Ashkenazim (Jews of Eastern European origin) the tradition is to wind the straps round the arm in an anti-clockwise direction, while the Sephardim (those of Spanish or Oriental origin) wind them clockwise. The Talmud stresses the importance of fulfilling this commandment, and it declares that even God lays tephillin. Among the Hasidim it is said that if only every male Jew would do his duty in this regard, then the Messiah would come.

A mezuzah is another small box containing parchment. The verses are Deuteronomy 6:4–9 and 11:13–21, the first two paragraphs of the Shema prayer. The word *Shaddai* (Almighty) is written on the back. The parchment is then inserted in a small opening in the box and it is nailed on the right-hand doorpost. It is placed about two-thirds of the way up in a slanting position so that the upper part points towards the house. Almost all Jews, if they are in any way observant, put mezuzahs on their front doors. The Strictly Orthodox put one on the doorpost of every room in the house except the bathroom and lavatory. Again, like laying phylacteries, this is a very old practice. A mezuzah was found in the excavations at Qumran, the site where the Dead Sea Scrolls were found.

Both the mezuzah and phylacteries are visible signs which remind the Jew of his obligation towards God. Every day he dedicates himself anew when he puts on his tephillin. Every time he enters or leaves his house, he is recalled to his awesome obligations as a member of God's Chosen People. The sages taught that the purpose of the mezuzah is to remind the Jew that all material possessions are a gift from God. All too often in the past, the mezuzah was seen as an amulet to ward off evil spirits. Some people went so far as to wear a mezuzah around the neck as a type of good luck charm. Today the mezuzah is perceived by the more secular as a badge of identity, a sign that the house, despite its similarities to its neighbours, is something special; it is a Jewish home. Among the pious, the mezuzah is a constant affirmation of the all-embracing nature of God's Torah and it is not uncommon to see the Orthodox reverently touch their mezuzahs, as they enter and leave their houses.

The laws of clothing

One of the most recognizable signs of masculine Orthodox dress is the skull-cap (*yarmulke* in Yiddish, *kippah* in Hebrew). In fact, the practice of wearing a skull-cap only goes back to about the twelfth century CE and may have been introduced to distinguish Jewish from Christian prayer. Christian men traditionally pray with their heads uncovered; Jews then came to wear a head-covering as a matter of custom. However, today all Orthodox men keep their heads covered at all times – to the extent that it is not uncommon to see a pious man take off his large outdoor hat and find that he is wearing a skull-cap underneath. Members of Conservative and Reform congregations generally wear a head-covering in the synagogue, but go about bare-headed on secular occasions.

According to the book of Leviticus, it is forbidden to cut the corners of the beard (19:27). Throughout the Middle Ages, it was the custom for Jewish men to wear beards, and the Talmud describes the beard as the 'ornament of the face'. Later the biblical verse was interpreted to mean that Jews should not shave, but it was permissible to clip facial hair. Today many Jewish men are clean-shaven; they dispose of their beards either by clipping with an electric razor or with a chemical depilatory. Among the Hasidim and the very Orthodox, the passage from Leviticus is also understood to mean that men should allow their side-locks to grow. These are known as *peot*, and are frequently seen on young boys. Adult men tend to curl the locks round and tuck them behind their ears so that they are almost invisible.

Another element of Orthodox appearance is fringes (*tzitzit*). According to the book of Numbers, God told the Israelites 'to make tassels on the corners of their garments ... and it shall be to you a tassel to look upon and remember all the commandments of the Lord' (15:37–8). Orthodox men wear an undergarment with fringes on the four corners; these are tied in a particular way to symbolize the numerical value of the name of God. Known as the *tallit katan*, the garment is largely hidden although the fringes are brought out above the trouser waistband and are discreetly tucked into a pocket. Similar fringes are put on the four corners of the prayer shawl (the *tallit gadol*) which is worn in the synagogue during the morning service. A special blessing is said when both the prayer shawl and the undergarment are put on each day.

Women's dress is characterized by modesty. Married women traditionally cover their heads and the Orthodox continue this practice either by wearing a wig or by swathing the head in a large scarf. Skirts cover the knee and sleeves the elbow. The non-Orthodox ignore these customs and, particularly in Israel, it is not unknown for the Strictly Orthodox to vent their disapproval on strange young women whom they perceive to be improperly dressed. A particular area of contention is the wearing of jeans. The book of Deuteronomy teaches that 'a woman shall not wear anything that pertains to a man, nor shall a man put on a woman's garment' (22:5). Thus any unisex garment is perceived as an abomination.

A final law concerning clothing is that of *shaatnes*, or forbidden cloth. The law states: 'You shall not wear a mingled stuff, wool and linen together' (Deuteronomy 22:11). This regulation is one of several laws against mixing. Vineyards should not be sown with two different types of seed and an ox and a donkey should not be yoked together at the plough. Today modern technology can be employed to determine the precise composition of fabrics, and there are several '*shaatnes* laboratories' which can carry out tests and certify the legality of a particular material. In any event the commandment is only understood to forbid the mingling of linen and wool. Any other combination, such as wool and acrylic or cotton and silk, is permissible. Again this law is ignored by the non-Orthodox.

In the past, Jews were all too often compelled by secular governments to wear distinctive emblems. From the seventh century CE, Muslim rulers insisted that Jews wear special clothing and the same provision was made by the Christian Church in the thirteenth century. The practice was revived by Hitler's Nazis in the Holocaust period, when all Jews were compelled to wear yellow Stars of David. Today, however, the vast majority of Jews are indistinguishable from the mass of the general population. Those who do wear distinctive dress, such as the skull-cap or fringes, do so solely as an expression of their personal religious convictions.

Forbidden foods

If there is a single factor which has kept the Jewish people separate from the other nations of the world, it is the food laws. Because certain foods are forbidden, because even permitted animals must be slaughtered in a particular way and because there can be no mixing of certain categories of food, observant Jews cannot eat in secular restaurants nor in the houses of gentile acquaintances. As the Jew Shylock puts it in Shakespeare's *Merchant of Venice*, 'I will buy with you, sell with you, talk with you, walk with you and so following; but I will not eat with you, drink with you nor pray with you.' In effect, all reciprocal socializing based on sharing food and drink is forbidden. For friends, Jews must turn to their own community.

According to the creation story in the book of Genesis, the earliest human beings were vegetarians: 'And God said: Behold I have given you every plant yielding seed which is upon the face of all the earth and every tree with seed in its fruit; you shall have them for food' (1:29). Only after the great flood did God allow Noah and his family to eat meat: 'Every moving thing that lives shall be food for you; and as I give you the green plants, I give you everything. Only you shall not eat flesh with its life, that is, its blood' (Genesis 9:3–4). Nonetheless the eating of meat is hedged about with many restrictions, and several authorities teach that in the days of the Messiah, both human beings and animals will return to vegetarianism.

In the first place, not all animals or birds may be eaten. The book of Deuteronomy specifies that for an animal to be permitted as food, it must both have a cloven hoof and chew the cud (14:6). Pigs are forbidden because they do not chew the cud; rabbits fail on both criteria and camel meat may not be consumed because the camel has a pad for a foot. Therefore the only animals commonly eaten are oxen, sheep, goats and deer. No rules are offered for birds, but the biblical list of forbidden species consists largely of birds of prey.

Then the creature must be slaughtered in a particular manner. Because of the prohibition against eating blood, the ritual involves getting rid of as much blood as possible from the carcass. A Jewish ritual slaughterer (*a shohet*) has to undergo considerable training. The knife must be perfectly smooth and razor-sharp. The creature is killed by a quick downward slicing of the throat. Then the body is suspended to drain off its blood.

After slaughter is completed, the carcass is inspected and if there is any evidence of internal injury or disease, then it is pronounced forbidden (*terefah*). It is frequently argued that the Jewish method of slaughter is the most painless possible. This was certainly the case in the past, but today some authorities on animal welfare argue that the modern practice of pre-stunning is more humane. Unfortunately, according to Jewish law, it is not possible to stun the animal or bird before slaughter since this would constitute a blemish and would render the carcass forbidden.

There are no rules for the slaughter of fish, but not all sea creatures may be eaten. According to Deuteronomy, 'Of all that are in the waters, you may eat these: whatever has fins and scales you may eat and whatever does not have fins and scales you shall not eat; it is unclean for you' (14:9). This means that all shellfish (oysters, crabs, lobsters, mussels, shrimps) are forbidden, as are eels and turtles. The roe of forbidden fish, like the eggs of forbidden birds, is also not permitted. However, Jews may eat honey, even though bees, in common with all other insects, are not to be consumed.

It is also not permitted to eat both meat foods and dairy products at the same meal. This prohibition grows out of the rabbinical interpretation of the verse, 'You shall not boil a kid in its mother's milk,' which appears no less than three times in the Pentateuch (in Exodus 23:19, 34:26 and Deuteronomy 14:21). This may have originally been designed to counter the pagan practice of seething a new-born creature in the milk of its own mother. However, it has been understood to mean that neither meat nor poultry may be mixed with milk or with anything made from milk. Again this ruling does not apply to fish. So a hamburger may not be served with cheese, nor chicken in a milky soup; on the other hand cod or haddock may be cooked in a creamy sauce.

The kosher kitchen

The laws of kashrut are the Jewish dietary laws. The term 'kosher' literally means 'fit' or suitable for consumption; kosher food, then, is food which is proper for Jews to eat. Today many mass-produced products carry a certificate guaranteeing kashrut. The Chief Rabbinate or national central authority organizes the award of these certificates. A whole bureaucracy of experts has grown up who inspect factories and slaughterhouses to ensure that the laws are kept in every particular. However, following the principle of where there are five Jews there are six opinions, this is not enough for some of the Strictly Orthodox. Many groups refuse to accept the word of the central authority, and they set up their own organizations and provide their own rival certificates.

Once an acceptable authority has been decided on, the housewife will set up her own kosher kitchen to ensure that the food is correctly prepared. The first necessity is to keep milk and meat foods completely separate. It is not enough to avoid serving them together. Minute particles of food can permeate crockery, cutlery and cooking utensils and can thus mingle during the process of preparation. To avoid this, the housewife has two completely different sets of plates and saucepans. There must even be separate washing-up bowls, draining boards and preparation areas. Today in an affluent household, it is not uncommon to see two sinks, two refrigerators and even two dishwashers. In effect there are two different kitchens.

If the kitchen is being set up from the beginning, this is not too complicated. Everything is completely new and there is no danger of cross-contamination. Even so, all the equipment must be taken to the ritual bath to be immersed before it is used. Problems arise if the household has not been particularly observant, but then has a change of heart – or if a group of observant Jews wants to hold a function in a hotel or banqueting hall which normally serves unkosher food. In such cases a kashrut inspector has to supervise the koshering of the kitchen. This can be done by burning off all the traces of food with a blow-torch and by immersing pots and silverware in huge vats of boiling water. It is a complicated and thorough process, but it is possible. Nothing, however, can be done about pottery and china since it would break if it were subjected to the necessary high temperature. New sets have to be brought.

Once meat is brought into the kitchen, it must undergo further treatment. In order to avoid the eating of blood, the meat must be soaked in clean water for thirty minutes. It is then thoroughly salted and put on a grooved board for an hour. The board must be placed on a slant to encourage drainage. Then the meat is rinsed several times in running water. An alternative method, which is more practical with such foods as liver, is to get rid of the blood by roasting it over an open flame. Today many kosher butchers sell meat already salted, but roasting remains an important task. Different communities have different customs for the time permitted between eating milk and meat products. Generally meat can be eaten, provided it is not part of the same meal, almost immediately after milk. The mouth must be rinsed with water or bread must be swallowed in between. But after the consumption of meat, it may be as much as six hours before dairy foods can be taken.

Keeping a kosher home is a serious commitment for a young couple. Because of the cost of inspection and the training required for ritual slaughter, kosher food is not cheap. There is no particular kosher cuisine. Food that is generally regarded as 'kosher-style', such as salt beef, dill cucumber, potato latkes (pancakes) and gefilte fish (fish dumplings) is merely the food of Eastern Europe. Oriental Jews tend to follow the cuisines of their own countries and it is quite possible to serve Chinese, Indian, Thai or Mexican food which is strictly kosher. New

York, for example, has an extraordinary array of kosher restaurants of many different types.

It is commonly argued that the laws of kashrut developed for considerations of health – that pork was forbidden because it was the host for tape-worm and so on. This explanation has no place in the traditional perceptions of the laws of kashrut. The laws were laid down by God for His people and that, for the Orthodox, is the end of the matter. In an observant home, every meal is a reminder of chosenness, a celebration of the unique relationship between God and the Jews. However, by no means all Jewish people keep kosher. This is an area where there are many degrees of observance. Some completely ignore the food laws; others avoid pork and shellfish, but eat everything else; others keep a kosher home but eat anything when they are out, and still others follow all the laws in their most minute detail.

Family values

In the modern world, the Jewish people are widely admired for their family values. It is said that the community has few broken families, low levels of delinquency, high standards of education and strong bonds between the generations. It is still true that, on average, Jewish children do better in school and are more likely to go on to tertiary education than their gentile counterparts. Sadly, at any rate among the non-Orthodox, rates of divorce increasingly parallel those of other communities and the demands of modern employment often force parents and adult children to live far apart. In the Dispersion, in this, as in many other matters, most Jews are becoming indistinguishable from their neighbours.

Nonetheless, the family circle remains important. Among the Orthodox, the roles of men and women remain very different. Because of her domestic duties, a woman is not expected to perform all the positive time-bound commandments. She does not have to wear fringes or lay phylacteries. She has no obligation to attend daily services and, if she does go, her presence does not count towards the necessary quorum. Her obligations are to care for the material needs of her family, to ensure that her children are educated and to encourage her husband to continue his studies. Men are commanded to love and respect their wives and there is no doubt that, within the family itself, the woman is extraordinarily influential. In the poular sphere this is reflected both in sentimental reminiscence ('My Yiddishe Momma') and in regular diatribes against the whole race of Jewish mothers (Philip Roth's *Portnoy's Complaint* is an obvious and notorious example).

Today many women are unhappy with this pattern. They feel that the whole role was imposed on them by men and they also want to make their mark beyond the home. It is no accident that many leading feminists have been of Jewish origin (Betty Friedan and Gloria Steinem spring to mind). The non-Orthodox have moved with the times. In both the Reform and the Conservative movements, women can be ordained as rabbis and can lead the synagogue services as cantors. In the secular sphere, most parents are keen that their daughters as well as their sons should achieve the highest educational standards. In the Dispersion, at any rate, young people are marrying later; there are many more single people and this lifestyle does not reflect traditional Jewish family values.

At the same time, the community is wistful about the old ways. Secular Jews look to the family lives of the Strictly Orthodox with their clearly demarcated areas of responsibility and their large numbers of children with a mixture of awe, disapproval and envy. As the modern secular husband examines his high-powered working wife and his one or two difficult adolescent children, the old ways can seem attractive. Nonetheless, for most they are unattainable. It would be nice to be honoured by one's offspring, to have a son who, as the Talmud puts it, does not contradict his father's words nor decide against his opinions. Regrettably, such a relationship goes against all modern ideas of child-rearing!

Other Jewish values are also admired by outsiders. The law insists on integrity in business as the mark of an upright man. The relationship between employer and employee must be one of mutual co-operation, fairness and trust. All Jews have a duty to support the poor and needy and to give regularly and generously to charity. This is still taken seriously and Jewish welfare organizations are, in general, efficiently run and well supported. Hospitality to the stranger is another obligation and most Jewish households entertain guests regularly, particularly on the festivals and for Sabbath dinner on Friday night. One Strictly Orthodox rabbi of the authors' acquaintance refuses to administer charity directly from his synagogue. If a needy person comes to his door, he or she is simply provided with the address list of all the members of the congregation. The rabbi knows that the stranger will be provided with food and shelter from one or other member of the community.

Judaism teaches that the upright person will speak the truth at all times; gossip and slander are to be deplored; animals must be treated with kindness and compassion and honest labour is to be commended. It is obvious that all is not as it should be in the world. The duty of the pious Jew is to start the work of repair and to restore again the peace created by God. At its best, the Jewish family is a microcosm of that ideal harmony and, as such, it is seen as the beginning of the healing process. As the liturgical grace after meals puts it: 'I have been young and now I am grown old, yet never have I seen a righteous man utterly forsaken ... The Eternal will give strength unto His people, the Eternal will bless His people with His peace.'[1]

13
Death and mourning

Care of the sick and dying

In the Mishnah, there is a well-known story about the great Rabbi Hillel (early first century CE). He was approached by a pagan man who wanted to convert to Judaism, but who insisted that he should be taught the whole Torah while standing on one leg. Hillel was not upset by this challenge. He said that whatever is hateful to yourself, you should not do to your fellow human beings, that this is the whole of the Torah and that all the rest is commentary. This remains the crucial ethical principle in the Jewish religion, and it is merely an elaboration of the biblical verse, 'You shall love your neighbour as yourself' (Leviticus 19:18).

The maxim is clearly illustrated in the law and practice concerning the sick and the dying. There is nothing so depressing as being ill all by oneself. Visiting the unwell is an important duty in the tradition and, in many communities, voluntary societies are set up to make sure that no one is overlooked. The Talmud teaches that 'whoever visits the sick causes him to recover'.[1] However, even with frequent visitors and with the best possible nursing, the life of each individual does eventually have to come to an end. Judaism has a great deal to say about death and dying.

First of all, the law is concerned to determine the exact point of death. In talmudic times it was believed that a person had died once there was no further sign of breathing. Today, with new methods of resuscitation, the problem is more complicated. Modern Orthodox authorities say either that life has ended when both breath and heartbeats stop or, alternatively, when there is evidence of brain-stem death. In any event, a person hovering between life and death is alive. Life is a gift from God and nothing must be done to hasten the end. However, it is permitted to pray for death to come in the case of an invalid who is in great pain, for whom there is no hope and who himself longs to die. At the same time, no medical effort may be spared to save one who is dying and Judaism is firmly opposed to any form of euthanasia. The two key scriptural texts in this regard are 'You shall not kill' (Exodus 20:13) and 'You shall not stand forth against the life of your neighbour' (Leviticus 19:16).

The tradition emphasizes that the utmost regard and consideration should be shown to the dying. They must be urged to make a final confession to God. At the same time it is important to avoid upsetting them and to keep the hope of life alive. To solve this dilemma, the Talmud suggests the following formula: 'Many have confessed, but have not died, but many who have not confessed have died. And there are many who are still walking about in the market place who have confessed. By the merit of your confession you shall live, because all who confess have a place reserved for them in the World-to-Come.' The formal words of confession are also laid down: 'I admit before You, God, my God and God of my ancestors, that my cure or my death are in Your hands ... If I die, may my death be an atonement for the sins transgressed and violated against You. And set my portion in the Garden of Eden, and let me merit the World-to-Come reserved for the righteous.' Then the prayer ends with the great declaration of the Jewish faith: 'Hear O Israel, the Lord our God, the Lord is One.' Ideally this statement of belief in God's unity will be the dying person's last words. All those present should pronounce the benediction, blessing God as the God of truth, and the relations should say the funeral prayer which accepts the finality of God's decrees and describes Him as the righteous judge.

As the last words of the dying imply, the very act of death can serve as a final atonement. The usual means by which sins are forgiven are by giving to charity, by doing acts of kindness and by fasting, particularly on the Day of Atonement. However, the twelfth-century philosopher Maimonides taught that there were some sins so dreadful that they could only be expiated by death; the desecration of God's name is an example of one such abomination. The process of death, then, can be offered as a final atonement for all wrongdoing and as the last means by which a broken relationship with God can be restored. A good and pious death will help the soul return to God its creator.

Preparing the body

According to Jewish law, the body must be buried as soon as possible after death – ideally on the same or the next day. It is considered discourteous to the corpse to delay matters; only if the relatives live very far away or the Sabbath intervenes is postponement permitted. Thus in the modern world, Jewish funerals require considerable organization on the part of the funeral director. If someone dies during the night, the likelihood is that the funeral will be scheduled for the next day. In the meantime, besides all the religious obligations, all the legal requirements must be fulfilled. A doctor must sign the death certificate; the burial permit must be procured; newspaper notices will probably need to be prepared; the cemetery must be contacted and the grave must be dug. These arrangements all have to be made in a very short space of time.

The great principle of dealing with the body is that the dead must be honoured. All the religious rituals are designed with this in mind. After the person has drawn his or her final breadth, the eyes and the mouth are closed and the body is placed on the floor covered with a sheet. It must not be left alone. Mirrors throughout the house are covered and any standing bowls of water are poured out. No one knows the origin of these customs. Meanwhile, a lighted candle is placed near the head of the body and the close family rend their clothes. Today this is a symbolic act. The mourner stands and makes a tear at least a hand-breadth across on the right side of his or her outer garment, generally on a lapel, while saying a blessing.

It is considered a *mitzvah* (a good deed) to sit with the body. Indeed, any action performed for the dead is regarded as particularly meritorious. This is because it is doing an act of kindness to someone who has no means of returning it. While the watcher sits, it is customary to read from the book of Psalms. In the modern world the preparations for burial are organized by the funeral director. Usually the body is taken from the house to the funeral parlour where it will be washed. Among the Orthodox this task is performed by a Chevra Kadisha, a burial society. This is made up of volunteers, a team of women for the female dead and a team of men for the male. Members of the team take it in turns to wash the body thoroughly in warm water. As they do this they may turn the corpse from side to side, but they may not turn it over with the face down because this would count as dishonouring the dead. Then the body is dressed in a simple white linen or cotton shroud. Among Orthodox Jews, in death everyone is equal and wealth or poverty no longer matter. If a man was a regular attender at synagogue and often wore his prayer shawl in life, then he is also buried in it. The custom is to make it ritually defective first, by cutting off one of its fringes. Then the body is placed in a simple pine coffin, because again this is not a time for the flaunting of worldly wealth. It is not part of the tradition to embalm the corpse or to display it in an open coffin.

The non-Orthodox do not necessarily follow all these proceedings. Within the community, in this, as in every other matter, there are wide differences in levels of observance. Many would not cover mirrors or rend their clothes. They would feel no obligation to sit with the body and they would be appalled by the idea of volunteer ritual washers. Some people want very elaborate coffins and still others insist on embalming. Perhaps the most crucial point of difference lies in the final disposal of the body. Traditionally Jews bury their dead in a Jewish cemetery. In the secular world cremation is gaining in popularity for aesthetic, economic and ecological reasons and the Jewish community is not immune to this trend. In view of the Holocaust when the bodies of so many millions of Jews were unceremoniously burned in mass ovens, many feel that cremation is not an appropriate option even for the most secular-minded. Nonetheless it is a choice that many people make and the modern Jewish funeral home will provide for it.

The funeral service

Different communities observe different customs when burying the dead. Nonetheless certain features are common to all Orthodox funerals. The general pattern involves the ritual rending of garments, the funeral procession into the cemetery, the eulogy either in the funeral chapel or by the grave and the special memorial prayers.

The rending of garments may be done just after the moment of death, as described previously, or just before the funeral itself. It is an ancient sign of mourning and it represents the torn and broken heart of the garment wearer. Only close relatives are expected to perform the ritual, namely husbands and wives, parents, children and siblings. If it takes place just before the funeral, then it is the rabbi conducting the service who makes the tear. The benediction accompanying it blesses God as the ruler of the universe and its true judge.

Then the rabbi leads the funeral procession to the cemetery. It is considered a good deed to escort the dead, and even those who are not going to the graveyard will follow the procession for a few steps. The custom is to stop either three or seven times along the way while reciting Psalm 91. This is to allow the mourners to express their grief. Psalm 91 is a song of comfort:

> He who dwells in the shadow of the Most High, who abides in the shadow of the Almighty, will say to the Lord, 'My refuge and my fortress: my God in whom I trust' ... Because you have made the Lord your refuge, the Most High your habitation, no evil shall befall you, no scourge come near your tent ... Because he cleaves to Me in love, I will deliver him; I will protect him because he knows My Name (1, 9, 10, 14).

In some communities Proverbs 31 or Psalm 16 is substituted if the corpse is a woman.

When the grave is reached, the coffin is lowered into it. The rabbi prays that the dead person may come to his or her rest in peace. Then the grave is filled. This is done by the adult males present, led by the chief mourners. The practice is that each man casts three shovelfuls of earth into the grave until it is covered. The spade may not be passed from hand to hand. It must be laid down on the ground and then picked up again. Meanwhile more prayers are read, probably including Psalm 91 again and, among Eastern European Jews, the prayer 'O God full of compassion ... May his [or her] resting place be the Garden of Eden. May the Compassionate One shelter him [or her] forever in His protective wings and may his [or her] soul be bound up in the bond of eternal life.'[2] Oriental Jews have their own special memorial prayer and they follow the custom of making seven circuits round the coffin before it is finally put in the ground.

The eulogy can take place either in the funeral chapel before the procession or at the graveside itself. There are extensive rules in the Talmud about praising the dead. The pious acts and virtues of the deceased should be emphasized as this will both comfort the bereaved and will serve as an edifying example to others. On the other hand, eulogies should not be so flattering that they undermine credibility. They are not given in the case of suicides or for those who have been excommunicated from the community (this last is very rare nowadays). Today, in the case of a secular Jew, all too often the rabbi did not know the deceased. In this event it is customary for a meeting to take place between the rabbi and the family beforehand to work out what to say.

Finally the Kaddish, an Aramaic prayer of praise to God, is recited. This is the traditional mourners' prayer and at the funeral an extended version is said which mentions God's resurrection of the dead and looks to the restoration of Jerusalem. Then all those present who are not members of the family form two lines. The family members pass between them and the guests make their condolences. The traditional words are 'May God comfort you among all the mourners of Zion and Jerusalem.' Before leaving the cemetery all participants wash their hands.

Dead bodies are traditionally regarded as the source of ritual impurity. As a result, people who believe themselves to be of priestly descent (Kohenim) must avoid all contact. They would never become funeral directors or volunteer their services to a burial society. They are forbidden to enter a cemetery, a funeral parlour or any enclosed space where a dead person is lying. An exception, however, is made when the corpse is that of an immediate relation. In general therefore the Kohenim do not attend funerals; they wait outside the chapel or the cemetery to offer their condolences to the family afterwards. The non-Orthodox who have rejected the priestly laws ignore these customs.

The laws of mourning

Once the funeral is over, the Orthodox family returns home to begin a seven-day period of mourning. This is known as sitting *shiva*. Before the funeral the mourners are exempt from the positive commandments; they are not expected to attend synagogue, to lay tephillin or to recite grace after meals. After the funeral, they must stay at home for seven days. During this time they are forbidden to go to work, to shave, to have their hair cut, to wear leather shoes or to use cosmetics, and they continue to wear their rent garments. It is the custom to keep the mirrors in the house covered and to light a special memorial candle. The family sits together on low stools and ideally the whole group – spouses, parents, children and siblings – remain in one place for the whole *shiva* period. Many family reconciliations have taken place during this enforced cloistering.

During this week, visitors from the community come to the house to offer their condolences. The first meal after the funeral is normally prepared by friends or neighbours so that the widow is not preoccupied with cooking and entertaining. It often contains eggs or round food – eggs because they are a symbol of new life and hope and round foods as a reminder of the wheel of fate in which life and death are part of a never-ending circle. The visitors are not expected to greet the bereaved; in fact, extending greeting is specifically forbidden to mourners during the seven days. Instead they sit down quietly with the family, sympathizing with their loss, sharing their tears and offering gentle words of consolation. In many (but not all) communities, it is the custom for visitors to bring food with them so there is always plenty to eat for the family and no domestic responsibilities.

Meanwhile the mourners should recite the mourners' Kaddish prayer three times each day to coincide with the daily services. This is essentially a declaration of God's glory:

Glorified and sanctified be God's great Name throughout the
world which He has created according to His will ... Blessed
and praised, glorified and exalted, extolled and honoured,
adored and praised be the Name of the Holy One, blessed be
He, beyond all the blessings and hymns, praises and consolation
that are ever spoken in the world. And let us say, Amen.

The Kaddish can only be recited when a quorum of ten adult
men is present so the quorum must come to the house of
mourning for the full week in the morning and in the evening.
Among the non-Orthodox, women also count towards the
quorum, and today, even in Orthodox circles, widows, daughters and sisters tend to say Kaddish with their male relatives. On
the Sabbath, it is customary for the family to leave the house and
go to synagogue. There they all enter the building together and
are greeted with the prayer of consolation, 'May God comfort
you among all the mourners of Zion and Jerusalem.' If a Jewish
holiday intervenes in the seven-day period, then the *shiva* is cut
short; if the funeral takes place during a holiday period, such as
the seasons of Passover or Tabernacles, *shiva* does not begin until
the festival is ended. This seems hard, but the principle is that
there must be no mourning during the holidays.

Shiva ends on the morning of the seventh day. Often the
rabbi or other leading member of the community will come to
the house to escort the mourners on their first walk outside.
Then, for the next thirty days, there is a time of lesser mourning. During this period, the family should still avoid shaving,
having their hair cut, attending parties or wearing new clothes.
But they go back to work and life begins to return to normality.

After this, in most communities, the time of mourning is
over, except in the case of parents. They must be mourned
for a year and during this time the children are still meant not
to shave or have their hair cut until urged to do so by their
friends.

The practice of sitting *shiva* is unique to the Jewish tradition and, from all accounts, it is a healing and beneficial custom. It gives the chance for friends and neighbours to do something concrete for the bereaved at a difficult time. Simply by sitting in silence, by quietly remembering the deceased or by distracting the mourner with local news, they are doing a real service. At the same time it gives the family a clear space of time to adjust to their new situation, to be surrounded by family and to be sustained by the love and concern of the community as a whole.

Memorials

For eleven months after the death of a parent, the Orthodox say Kaddish for the deceased. Since it can only be said in a quorum of ten adult men, this is an important factor in ensuring that synagogue daily services do occur every day. The regular worshippers are joined by the mourners. It is hoped that by going so regularly to synagogue, the mourners too will become regular worshippers. In any event, if the synagogue has managed to provide nine other grown men so the mourner can fulfil his duties, then the mourner is under a certain obligation to become part of the quorum when others need to mourn.

In Orthodox circles, the Kaddish is traditionally only said by men; there is a problem if the family only contains daughters. If a woman's mother has died and there are no brothers, perhaps her husband, as son-in-law, will take on the duty of saying Kaddish. An alternative solution is to hire a member of the congregation to attend daily services and to say the prayer on her behalf. Normally such a person would be on the staff of a talmudic academy and the payments would be a contribution to the academy's funds. If the woman decides to attend the daily services herself, there are no objections in Jewish law, but, at least among the Orthodox, she will not count towards the quorum.

Finally, every year the dead person is remembered on the Hebrew date of his or her death. This death anniversary is known as the Yahrzeit and rituals associated with it go back to the fifteenth century. It was believed that if the mourner said Kaddish on every Yahrzeit, this would ensure that the soul of the dead would ascend to the higher spheres. The practice is to light a memorial candle for the full day (which, as is the Jewish custom, begins the evening before). In some communities, Yahrzeit is kept as a fast day and frequently a visit to the grave is made. On the Sabbath before the Yahrzeit, a memorial prayer is chanted in the synagogue, and on the Yahrzeit itself, the mourner is called upon to lead the daily services. Because it is likely, in a large congregation, that many Yahrzeits fall each week, it is customary to recite the memorial prayer directly after the Torah reading on the Sabbath afternoon in commemoration of them all. Thus, in the Jewish tradition, the memory of those who have died is kept alive in the minds and hearts of those who loved them by regular annual rituals.

Non-Orthodox Jews do not observe all these customs. Nonetheless the practices of saying Kaddish, at least occasionally, and lighting a memorial candle are widespread in the community. It clearly answers a deeply-felt need. In many non-Orthodox synagogues, the practice is for the entire congregation to say the mourners' Kaddish every week. This is to remember the victims of the Nazi Holocaust. Whole families and communities were snuffed out in Hitler's concentration camps. No one was left to mourn them, to say Kaddish for them or to remember their Yahrzeit. The congregational Kaddish is a small step in remedying this.

Because Jews are buried, their graves can be visited and the graves are generally marked with tombstones. In Israel it is the custom to set the tombstone thirty days after the death, but in the Dispersion it is usual to wait a year. Among the Ashkenazim (the Eastern Europeans) tombstones are placed vertically at the head of the grave while the Sephardim (the Orientals) lay a horizontal stone over the whole grave. The setting of the gravestone is accompanied by a ceremony which usually includes the recitation of verses from Psalm 119, the prayer 'O God full of compassion ...' and the mourners' Kaddish. Different communities use different tombstone designs. Normally the inscription is in Hebrew and, after the name of the deceased, a prayer is chiselled such as 'May his memory be a blessing' or 'May she find rest in Eden'. There may also be a design, such as an incomplete pillar or a chopped-down tree. If the dead person was of priestly descent, sometimes hands are carved, lifted in the priestly blessing. It is a pious duty to visit the graves of loved ones or of famous teachers. In many communities, it is usual for the visitor to leave a pebble on the grave as a sign of respect. When looking round old Jewish graveyards, particularly on the tombs of eminent men, it is not uncommon to see sizeable piles of stones, showing that these lives have not been forgotten.

The Holocaust has created the need for a different sort of memorial. In the death camps, the bodies were shovelled into crematoria ovens or bulldozed into mass graves. Since then world Jewry has ensured that memorials have been built for the nameless victims. Famous artists have been employed and many of these tributes are unbearably moving. In addition, the dead are commemorated in Holocaust museums. These tell the full story of the persecution and annihilation of the Jews of Europe between 1933 and 1945. They were built both to honour the memory of the dead and also to ensure that such a calamity is never allowed to occur again.

Afterword

Judaism is not a static tradition. The Orthodox may continue to believe that God gave the 613 commandments to Moses on Mount Sinai, that they are perfect and that they can never be altered. At the same time, even the most holy recognizes that modern life throws up new situations and that the law must be interpreted anew to meet these challenges. It must be continually studied and pondered if it is to continue to provide guidance in all the contingencies that face human beings today. Thus legal experts are devoting themselves to the problems of medical ethics which arise out of new techniques and discoveries; they are confronting the results of faster and cheaper travel and they are considering the implications of instant world-wide electronic communications.

Among the non-Orthodox, it has always been accepted that Jewish law can be adapted and changed in the face of modern life. For many the effect of this is that their lives are nearly identical with those of their non-Jewish neighbours. They live in the same neighbourhoods; they work in the same offices; their children attend the same schools and their families enjoy the same entertainments. This may well be the first step in the loosening of the ties of the twenty-first-century Jew with the religion of his ancestors.

Today in the Dispersion, the Jewish community is facing many problems. The rate of intermarriage seems to increase every year; the feminist revolution has undermined the traditional position of Jewish women; some young people are avoiding family life altogether and choosing an alternative lifestyle and secular society becomes ever more unspiritual and materialistic.

Even in Israel, Jews are not immune from these trends. Despite the influence of the Strictly Orthodox, many Israelis want to have little to do with organized religion. Their identity as Jews rests entirely on their political nationality and they are impatient with the perceived fanaticism of their co-religionists.

Jewish survival is very much on the agenda. Some commentators believe that outside the Strictly Orthodox ghetto, there will be no more pious generations. Others are more hopeful. The Jews have existed as a separate ethnic and religious group for more than three thousand years and their present problems should be seen as no more than short-term difficulties. Whatever the future, those on both sides of the debate know that the Jewish influence on world civilization has been immense. Through its daughter religions, Christianity and Islam, a large proportion of the world's teeming population are monotheists. The Jewish Sabbath, the idea of a weekly day of rest, has become part of the rhythm of modern consciousness and the Jewish ethical ideals of justice, integrity and loving-kindness have infiltrated every civilization. By any reckoning it is a noble achievement.

At the same time the task is not yet complete. There remains much in the world which needs repair and restoration. The messianic era is not yet with us. Arguably there is still the need for the pious Jew who persists in his daily prayers and who continues to make the intercession, 'May He who maketh peace in the high heavens, grant peace unto us and unto all Israel. And say ye, Amen.'

Notes

Chapter 1

1. Solomon ibn Gabirol, trans. B. Lewis, *The Kingly Crown*, London, 1961.
2. *Exodus Rabbah* on Exodus 5:1–3. For an introduction to Midrash, see H. I. Strack and G. Stemberger, trans. M. Bockmuehl, *Introduction to the Talmud and Midrash*, Edinburgh, 1991.
3. Bahya ibn Asher ibn Halawa, *Commentary on the Pentateuch*, first published Naples, 1492.
4. J. H. Hertz, ed., *Authorised Daily Prayer Book*, London, 1947.
5. H. Danby, trans., Akiva in the *Mishnah*, Oxford, 1933.
6. Levi Yitzhak of Berditchev, *Kaddish*. See Martin Buber, *Tales of the Hasidim*, New York, 1991.
7. J. H. Hertz, ed., *Authorised Daily Prayer Book*, London, 1947.

Chapter 2

1. J. H. Hertz, ed., *Authorised Daily Prayer Book*, London, 1947.
2. Ibid.
3. Moses Maimonides, 'The Thirteen Principles of the Jewish Faith' in J. H. Hertz, ed., *Authorised Daily Prayer Book*, London, 1947.
4. J. H. Hertz, ed., *Authorised Daily Prayer Book*, London, 1947.
5. Ibid.
6. Ibid.

Chapter 3

1. H. Danby, trans., Kiddushin III in the *Mishnah*, Oxford, 1933.
2. Federation of Humanistic Judaism, *Manifesto*, Detroit, 1986.

Chapter 4

1. J. H. Hertz, ed., *Authorised Daily Prayer Book*, London, 1947.
2. Judah Halevi, trans. N. Salaman, *Shirei Ziyyon*, London, 1924.
3. Theodor Herzl, trans. S. d'Avigdor, *The Jewish State*, London, 1955.
4. Isaac Mayer Wise, cited in W. Laqueur, *A History of Zionism*, New York, 1972.
5. Shalom Dov Schneersohn, cited in L. Jacobs, 'Zionism', in *The Jewish Religion*, Oxford, 1995.
6. The Central Council of American Rabbis, *The San Francisco Platform*, New York, 1976.
7. Emil Fackenheim, *God's Presence in History*, New York, 1972.
8. Ibid.

Chapter 5

1. Moses Maimonides, 'The Thirteen Principles of the Jewish Faith', in J. H. Hertz, ed., *Authorised Daily Prayer Book*, London, 1947.
2. Pittsburgh Platform, cited in W. Gunther Plaut, *The Growth of Reform Judaism*, New York, 1965.
3. Columbus Platform, cited in W. Gunther Plaut, *The Growth of Reform Judaism*, New York, 1965.
4. Karl Schmidt and Martin Buber, *Theologische Blaetter* 12, 1933. See M. Friedman, *Martin Buber: The Life of Dialogue*, NP, 1955.
5. J. H. Hertz, ed., *Authorised Daily Prayer Book*, London, 1947.
6. W. Gunther Plaut, *The Growth of Reform Judaism*, New York, 1965.

7. For a flavour of the Talmud, see Norman Soloman, *The Talmud*, London, 2009.
8. Moses Maimonides, 'The Thirteen Principles of the Jewish Faith', in J. H. Hertz, ed., *Authorised Daily Prayer Book*, London, 1947.
9. From the Talmud – see note 7 above.
10. Ibid.
11. Kaufmann Kohler, *Jewish Theology*, NP, 1968.
12. Moses Luzzatto, *The Path of the Upright*, NP, 1936.

Chapter 6

1. Joseph Caro, *Shulhan Arukh*. Only parts have been translated into English. For a flavour, see S. Ganzfried, trans. H. E. Goldin, *Code of Jewish Law*, New York, 1961.
2. Adolf Hitler, trans. R. Manheim, *Mein Kampf*, Boston, 1973.
3. *Nostra Aetate*, cited in 'Towards Reconciliation', in Dan Cohn-Sherbok, *The Crucified Jew*, London, 1992.

Chapter 7

1. J. H. Hertz, ed., *Authorised Daily Prayer Book*, London, 1947.
2. Deuteronomy 6:4–9 in J. H. Hertz, ed., *Authorised Daily Prayer Book*, London, 1947.
3. J. H. Hertz, ed., *Authorised Daily Prayer Book*, London, 1947.
4. Ibid.
5. Ibid.

Chapter 8

1. *Haggadah of Passover*, introduced by Louis Finkelstein, New York, 1942.
2. J. H. Hertz, ed., *Authorised Daily Prayer Book*, London, 1947.

Chapter 9

1. Moses Maimonides, trans. C. B. Chavel, *Mishneh Torah*, 2 vols., New York, 1967.

Chapter 10

1. J. H. Hertz, ed., *Authorised Daily Prayer Book*, London, 1947.
2. From 'The Ethics of the Fathers', in J. H. Hertz, ed., *Authorised Daily Prayer Book*, London, 1947.

Chapter 12

1. J. H. Hertz, ed., *Authorised Daily Prayer Book*, London, 1947.

Chapter 13

1. For a flavour of the Talmud, see A. Cohen, *Everyman's Talmud*, New York, 1975.
2. J. H. Hertz, ed., *Authorised Daily Prayer Book*, London, 1947.

Glossary

Adar   the twelfth month in the Jewish year

Adonai   the Lord, a traditional name of God

Agudat Israel   international organization of Orthodox Jews

agunah   a tied woman; a woman who is separated from her husband but is neither a widow nor divorced

Alenu   prayer proclaiming the greatness of God

Amidah   a prayer consisting of eighteen benedictions which is recited standing

Aramaic   the language of the Talmud

Ashkenazim   Jews of Eastern European origin

assimilation   the loss of Jewish identity in mainstream culture

Av   the fifth month in the Jewish year

9 Av   fast day commemorating the destruction of the Jerusalem Temple

Baal   the god of the Canaanites

bar mitzvah   the coming-of-age ceremony for Jewish boys

bat   daughter of

bat mitzvah   the coming-of-age ceremony for Jewish girls

Belz   a sect of the Hasidim

ben   son of

berit milah   the covenant of circumcision

brit   the circumcision

Canaan   the land promised by God to the Jewish people

Canaanites   the original inhabitants of the Promised Land

cantor   the leader of the synagogue musical liturgy

Chevra Kadisha   voluntary burial society

Christ   Greek translation of the Hebrew word for Messiah

code   a compilation of Jewish law

confirmation   graduation service from synagogue religion school

Conservative   modified reformist religious movement within Judaism

cubit   approximately eighteen inches

Days of Awe   the New Year, the Day of Atonement and the days between them

Days of Penitence   Days of Awe

Dispersion   the Jewish communities outside Israel

El Elyon   God Most High, a traditional name of God

Elohim   God, a traditional name for the Almighty

El Olam   Eternal God, a traditional name for God

El Shaddai   God Almighty, a traditional name of God

Elul   the sixth month of the Jewish year

Enlightenment   the secular and liberal intellectual movement of the late eighteenth/early nineteenth centuries

Essenes a first-century ascetic sect

fast of Av see 9 Av

fast of Gedaliah fast commemorating the death of Gedaliah in 586 BCE

fast of Tammuz fast commemorating the breaching of the walls of Jerusalem in CE 70

fast of Tevet fast commemorating the Babylonian siege of Jerusalem in 587 BCE

Garden of Eden Heaven

gentile non-Jew

ger stranger (non-Jew)

get religious divorce

God-fearer gentile sympathetic to Judaism in the ancient world

Golden Calf the idol set up by Aaron in the wilderness

Great Hoshanah the seventh day of the feast of Tabernacles

Haggadah order of service of the Passover meal

Halakhah Jewish law

Hallel Psalms 113–18

Hamantashen cakes eaten at the feast of Esther

Hanukkah the festival of lights celebrating the victory of the Maccabees in the second century BCE

haroset a mixture eaten at Passover symbolizing mortar

Ha-Shem the Name, a traditional name of God

Hasidim a mystical religious movement which emerged in eighteenth-century Eastern Europe

Havdalah ceremony concluding the Sabbath

High Priest the senior priest who served in the Jerusalem Temple

Holocaust the Nazi destruction of European Jewry in the 1940s

Holy of Holies the central shrine of the Jerusalem Temple

huppah marriage canopy

idolatry worship of man-made gods

intermarriage marriage between Jew and gentile

Israel the Jewish people, the Jewish State created in 1948

Israelite member of the Jewish people, usually in the biblical period

Iyyar the second month of the Jewish year

JHWH the sacred name of God which is never pronounced

Kaddish doxology concluding the sections of the liturgical service, regularly said by mourners

kashrut the Jewish food laws

ketubah marriage contract

Ketuvim writings, the third section of the Bible after Torah and prophets

kippah skull-cap worn by observant Jewish men

Kislev ninth month of the Jewish year

Kohen hereditary priest

kolel   advanced talmudic academy

Kol Nidre   evening of the Day of Atonement

kosher   in accord with the laws of kashrut

Lag ba-Omer   scholars' feast celebrated on 18 Iyyar

Law of Return   Israeli law permitting all Jews to become Israeli citizens

Lubavitcher   sect of the Hasidim

lulav   bundle of palm, myrtle and willow waved on the Festival of Tabernacles

mamzer   one born as the result of an incestuous or adulterous union

Maoz Tsur   hymn sung on the festival of Hanukkah

Masorti   a modified reform movement, equivalent to Conservative Judaism

Matzot   unleavened bread

Mazal tov   good luck

Messiah   God's long-awaited anointed king who will restore the world to rights

mezuzah   parchment scroll attached to the doorpost

midrash   commentary on the biblical text

mikveh   ritual bath

Mishnah   Oral Law, the collection of oral law compiled in the second century CE

Mishneh Torah   the code of law compiled by Maimonides in the twelfth century CE *mitzvah* good deed

Mizrachi party of Orthodox Zionists

mohel performer of ritual circumcisions

musar ethics

neo-Orthodox a modernist movement within Orthodoxy

Neviim prophets, the second section of the Bible after Torah and before Ketuvim

New Year the beginning of the religious year on 1 Tishri, a solemn feast

New Year for Trees agricultural festival celebrated on 15 Shevat

Nisan the first month of the Jewish year

Nostra Aetate Papal pronouncement exonerating the Jewish people of the death of Jesus

omer one tenth of a measure of barley brought as an offering to the Temple

Oral Law the discussion and interpretation of the Written Law

Orthodox traditional Judaism, involving belief in the divine origin of the Torah

Passover spring festival celebrating the biblical liberation from Egypt

Patriarchs the ancestors of the Jews, Abraham, Isaac and Jacob

Pentateuch the first five books of the Hebrew scriptures

peot side-curls

Pesah   Passover

Pharisee   member of a religious sect of the Second Temple era

pidyon ha-ben   redemption of the first-born

Progressive   non-Orthodox, equivalent of Reform

Promised Land   land promised by God to the Israelites, Canaan

proselyte   convert

Purim   feast of Esther

rabbi   a learned man who has received ordination to preach and teach

Rav   Babylonian title for a Jewish scholar in the early Rabbinic period

Reconstructionist   a modernist movement which teaches that Judaism is an evolving historical civilization

Reform   a modernist movement which emphasizes the prophetic nature of the Jewish tradition

Rosh Hashanah   the Jewish New Year, the start of the Ten Days of Awe

Sabbath   the seventh day of the week, the day of rest

Sadducee   sect of hereditary priests in the Second Temple period

sandak   one who holds the baby during circumcision

Satmar   Hasidic sect

scapegoat   sin-offering sent out into the wilderness on Yom Kippur in the Temple period

scroll   rolled parchment on which the Torah or other sacred book is written

Seder   order of service particularly at Passover

Seleucids   foreign rulers of Palestine in the third and second centuries BCE

Sephardim   Jews of Spanish or Oriental origin

shaatnes   forbidden mixture of linen and wool

Shaddai   Almighty, a name of God

shammash   synagogue beadle

Shavuot   the summer festival of Weeks

shekel   ancient coin

Shema   central prayer of the liturgy affirming God's oneness

Shemini Atzeret   eighth day of the feast of Tabernacles

Sheol   shadowy realm of the dead

Shevat   eleventh month of the Jewish calendar

shewbread   bread laid out on the altar in the Temple

shiva   seven-day mourning period

Shivan   third month of the Jewish year

shofar   ram's horn, which is blown like a trumpet

shohet   ritual slaughterer

Shulhan Arukh   code of Jewish law compiled by Joseph Caro in the sixteenth century

Simhat Torah   final day of the festival of Tabernacles

Strictly Orthodox   completely faithful to the strict interpretation of the law *sukkah* booth in which Jews live during the feast of Tabernacles

Sukkot feast of Tabernacles

synagogue house of worship

tabernacle portable shrine used by the Israelites in the wilderness, hut built for dwelling in during the festival of Tabernacles

tallit gadol prayer shawl

tallit katan fringed undergarment

Talmud collection of oral law and commentary compiled in the fifth century in Palestine and the sixth century in Babylonia

Tammuz fourth month of the Jewish calendar

17 Tammuz fast commemorating the success of the Babylonian siege of Jerusalem in the sixth century BCE

Tanakh Hebrew scriptures

Temple magnificent central shrine in Jerusalem

Ten Commandments ten laws given by God to Moses as recorded in Exodus 20

tephillin phylacteries

terefah not kosher

Tevet tenth month in the Jewish calendar

10 Tevet fast commemorating the Babylonian siege of Jerusalem in the sixth century BCE

Tishah b'Av see 9 Av

Tishri seventh month in the Jewish calendar

Torah teaching of God to the Jews

tsaddik hereditary Hasidic leader

Twelve Tribes descendants of the twelve sons of the patriarch Jacob (Israel)

tzitzit see *tallit katan*

unleavened bread bread baked without a raising agent and eaten at Passover

Written Law the 613 commandments of the Pentateuch

Yahrzeit death anniversary of parent, spouse, child or sibling

yarmulke see kippah

yeshiva talmudic academy

Yiddish language of Eastern European Jews

Yiddishkeit Eastern European Jewish civilization

Yom Kippur Day of Atonement, the most solemn day of the Jewish year

Zion Jerusalem

Zionist person dedicated to restoring the Promised Land to the Jewish people

Further reading

Chapter 1

Samuel S. Cohon, *Jewish Theology: A Historical and Systematic Interpretation of Judaism and its Foundations.* Assen, 1971.

Louis Jacobs, *A Jewish Theology.* New York, 1973.

Kaufmann Kohler, *Jewish Theology Systematically Arranged* (with new material by Joseph L. Blau). New York, 1968.

Alan Unterman, *Jews: Their Religious Beliefs and Practices.* Sussex, 1999.

Chapter 2

Arthur A. Cohen and Paul Mendes Flohr, eds., *Contemporary Religious Thought.* New York, 1987.

Louis Jacobs, *God, Torah, Israel: Traditionalism Without Fundamentalism.* Cincinnati, 1990.

Norbert M. Samuelson, *Revelation and the God of Israel.* Cambridge, 2002.

Solomon Schechter, *Some Aspects of Rabbinic Theology.* New York, 1961.

Chapter 3

David Ariel, *What Do Jews Believe?: The Spiritual Foundations of Judaism.* New York, 1995.

Reuven P. Bulka, ed., *Dimensions of Orthodox Judaism.* New York, 1983.

Neil Gilman, *Conservative Judaism.* West Orange, NJ, 1993.

Michael A. Meyer, *Response to Modernity: A History of the Reform Movement in Judaism*. Oxford, 1998.

Chapter 4

Dan Cohn-Sherbok, David El-Alami, *The Palestine–Israeli Conflict*. Oxford, 2009.

Marc Ellis, *Judaism Does Not Equal Israel: The Rebirth of the Jewish Prophetic*. New York, 2009.

Arthur Hertzberg, *The Zionist Idea: A Historical Analysis and Reader*. New York, 1959.

Zvi Sobel and Benjamin Beit-Hallahmi, eds., *Tradition, Innovation, Conflict: Jewishness and Judaism in Contemporary Israel*. Albany, NY, 1991.

Chapter 5

L. Ginzberg, *Legends of the Jews*. Philadelphia, 1954.

Louis Jacobs, *Principles of the Jewish Faith*. London, 1964.

Jonathan Sacks, *One People? Tradition, Modernity and Jewish Unity*. London, 1993.

Rifat Sonsino, Daniel B. Syme, *What Happens After I Die?: Jewish Views of Life After Death*. New York, 1990.

Chapter 6

Max Eichorn, ed., *Conversion to Judaism: A History and Analysis*. New York, 1965.

Jacob Katz, *Exclusiveness and Tolerance*. Oxford, 1961.

Norman Soloman, *Judaism and World Religion*. London, 1992.

Robert Wistrich, *Anti-Semitism: The Longest Hatred*. London, 1991.

Chapter 7

Israel Abrahams, *A Companion to the Authorized Prayer Book.* New York, 1966.

Hayim Halevy Donin, *To Pray as a Jew: A Guide to the Prayer Book and the Synagogue Service.* New York, 1991.

Solomon Goldman, *A Guide to the Sabbath.* London, 1961.

Isaac Levy, *The Synagogue: Its History and Foundation.* London, 1963.

Chapter 8

Abraham Bloch, *The Biblical and Historical Background of the Jewish Holy Days.* New York, 1978.

Philip Goodman, *A Passover Anthology.* Philadelphia, 1961.

Irving Greenberg, *The Jewish Way: Living the Holidays.* New York, 1998.

S. J. Zevin, trans. Meir Fox-Ashri, *The Festivals in Halakhah.* New York, 1981.

Chapter 9

Philip Goodman, *The Rosh Hashanah Anthology.* Philadelphia, 1973.

Philip Goodman, *The Yom Kippur Anthology.* Philadelphia, 1971.

Hayim Schauss, *The Jewish Festivals: A Guide to Their History and Observance.* New York, 1996.

Chaim Pearl, *Minor Festivals and Fasts.* London, 1963.

Chapter 10

Rela M. Geffen (ed.), *Celebration and Renewal: Rites of PAssage in Judaism. Philadelphia,* 1993.

Isaac Klein, *A Guide to Jewish Religious Practice.* New York, 1979.

Norman Lamm, *Torah Ummadah: The Encounter of Religious*

Learning and World Knowledge in the Jewish Tradition. London, 1990.

Moira Paterson, ed., *The Bar Mitzvah Book*. London, 1975.

Chapter 11

William B. Helmreich, *The World of the Yeshiva*. New York, 1982.

Maurice Lamm, *The Jewish Way in Love and Marriage*. New York, 1991.

Louis Jacobs, *A Tree of Life: Diversity, Flexibility and Creativity in Jewish Law*. Oxford, 1984.

Isaac Klein, *A Guide to Jewish Religious Practice*. New York, 1979.

Chapter 12

Blu Greenberg, *How to Run a Traditional Jewish Household*. New York, 1983.

Richard Siegel, Michael Strassfield, Sharon Strassfield, *The Jewish Catalog*. Philadelphia, 1973.

Daniel Syme, The Jewish Home: A Guide for Jewish Living. New York, 2003.

Susannah Heschel, *On Being a Jewish Feminist*. New York, 1995.

Rabbi S. Wagschal, *A Practical Guide to Kashruth*. Gateshead, 1972.

Chapter 13

Hayim H. Donin, *To Be A Jew: A Guide to Jewish Observance in Contemporary Life*. New York, 1991.

Immanuel Jacobovits, *Jewish Medical Ethics*. New York, 1959.

Maurice Lamm, *Jewish Way in Death and Mourning*. New York, 1972.

Jack Riemer, ed., *Jewish Reflections on Death*. New York, 1974.

Index

A Beginner's Guide to The Middle East

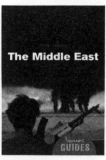

9781851686759
£9.99/ $14.95

This compact book by the University of Oxford's leading expert is stuffed with historical background, real-life examples, profiles of key figures from Nasser to Gadaffi, and even popular jokes from the area. *The Middle East: A Beginner's Guide* will captivate tourists, students, and the interested general reader alike.

"Masterly. A comprehensive and succinct overview." **Hugh Pope** – Former Middle East Correspondent for *Reuters, Wall Street Journal,* and the *Independent*

"The best book on the modern Middle East. Perfect not only for students but for any reader. It is balanced, authoritative and easy to follow. A perfect introduction to this troubled region." **Christopher Catherwood** – Author of *A Brief History of the Middle East*

PHILIP ROBINS is Reader in Middle East Politics at the University of Oxford. He is the author of *A History of Jordan* and has previously worked as a journalist for the BBC and the *Guardian*.

Browse further titles at
www.oneworld-publications.com

A Beginner's Guide to Christianity

Keith Ward

Christianity

Beginners
GUIDES

978-1-85168-539-4
£9.99/14.95

Renowned theologian and
bestselling author Keith Ward
provides an original and
authoritative introduction for
those seeking a deeper understanding of this complex
faith.

"Well ordered and clearly written. Will quickly become a standard
textbook." *Theology*

"An articulate presentation of diverse approaches to Christianity's
central concerns ... highly recommended." *Library Journal*

KEITH WARD is Professor of Divinity at Gresham College,
London and Regius Professor of Divinity Emeritus, at the
University of Oxford. A Fellow of the British Academy and an
ordained priest in the Church of England, he has authored many
books on the topics of Christianity, faith, and science including the best-selling *God: A Guide for the Perplexed* and *The Case for
Religion*, both published by Oneworld.

Browse further titles at
www.oneworld-publications.com

Beginners
GUIDES

A Beginner's Guide to Philosophy of Religion

Assuming no prior knowledge of philosophy from the reader, Taliaferro provides a clear exploration of the discipline, introducing a wide range of philosophers and covering the topics of morality and religion, evil, the afterlife, prayer, and miracles.

9781851686506
£9.99/ $14.95

"Brimming with arguments, the material is cutting edge, and the selection of topics is superb."
J.P. Moreland – Professor of Philosophy, St Olaf College, Minnesota

"Covers all the most important issues in a way that is always fair-minded, and manages to be accessible without over-simplifying" **John Cottingham** – President of the British Society for the Philosophy of Religion and Professor Emeritus of Philosophy, Reading University

CHARLES TALIAFERRO is Professor of Philosophy at St. Olaf College, Minnesota, USA. He is the author or editor of numerous books on the philosophy of religion including as co-editor of *The Blackwell Companion to Philosophy of Religion*.

Browse further titles at
www.oneworld-publications.com

A Beginner's Guide to The Buddha

978-1-85168-601-8
£9.99/ $14.95

In this authoritative biography, John Strong presents the Buddha's story the way Buddhists have told it – from accounts of his previous lives, and the story of his birth and upbringing, through to his enlightenment, deathbed deeds, and ongoing presence in the relics that he left behind.

"Among the many biographies of the Buddha available to the general reader, John Strong's remains the best. It draws from a vast body of sources with sensitivity and insight to paint a fascinating portrait of a towering figure." **Donald S. Lopez** – Arthur E. Link Distinguished University Professor of Buddhist and Tibetan Studies, University of Michigan

"Strong's book is clearly the best available 'Guide for Beginners'." **Frank Reynolds** – Professor Emeritus of History of Religions and Buddhist Studies, University of Chicago

JOHN S. STRONG is Charles A. Dana Professor of Religious Studies at Bates College in Maine, USA. He is the author of four other books on Buddhism.

Browse further titles at
www.oneworld-publications.com

A Beginner's Guide to Daoism

978-1-85168-566-0
£9.99/ $14.95

This informative book will prove invaluable not only to students, but also to general readers who wish to learn more about the origins and nature of a profound tradition, and about its role and relevance in our fast-moving, twenty-first-century existence.

"In this short volume, the author gives his readers not the last word on Daoism but invaluable handles 'to develop your own understanding' of this rich and complex tradition." *China Review International*

"Just the introductory text we have been waiting for – thoroughly up-to-date, admirably well written, and with an intelligent, and freshly different, thematic organization." **N.J. Girardo** – University Distinguished Professor, Lehigh University

JAMES MILLER is Associate Professor of Chinese Religions at Queen's University, Canada. He is the editor of *Chinese Religions in Contemporary Societies,* and has studied and worked extensively in the Far East.

Browse further titles at
www.oneworld-publications.com

A Beginner's Guide to The Qur'an

Drawing on both contemporary and ancient sources, Esack outlines the key themes and explains the historical and cultural context of this unique work whilst examining its content, language, and style, and the variety of approaches used to interpret it.

978-1-85168-624-7
£9.99/ $14.95

"Extremely learned yet accessible, with fascinating insights on virtually every page. Especially useful for those new to the study of Islam, or newly interested in their inherited Islam. Its clarity makes it suitable for undergraduates but its sophistication makes it of interest to graduates as well." **Tamara Sonn** – Kenan Professor of Humanities at the College of William and Mary, Virginia

"No one has placed the Noble Qur'an more fully in its historical and contemporary context. Esack's is a user's guide for all users, and it should enjoy a long shelf life as the most accessible, and informative, introduction to God's Word in Arabic." **Bruce Lawrence** – Nancy and Jeffrey Marcus Professor of Religion, Duke University

FARID ESACK has an international reputation as a Muslim scholar, speaker, and human rights activist. He has lectured widely on religion and Islamic Studies and also served as a Com missioner for Gender Equality in Nelson Mandela's government.

Browse further titles at
www.oneworld-publications.com